AF413650

Roman Military History

An Enthralling Guide to Battle Tactics, Empire Expansion, and the Might of the Roman Legions

Free limited time bonus

Stop for a moment. We have a free bonus set up for you. The problem is this: we forget 90% of everything that we read after 7 days. Crazy fact, right? Here's the solution: we've created a printable, 1-page pdf summary for this book that you're reading now. All you have to do to get your free pdf summary is to go to the following website:

https://livetolearn.lpages.co/enthrallinghistory/

Or, Scan the QR code!

Once you do, it will be intuitive. Enjoy, and thank you!

Table of Contents

Introduction

The Roman army traces its origins to the founding of Rome in 753 BCE. The history of the Roman state is inextricably tied to the history of the Roman military; the two could not exist without one another. From humble beginnings as a citizen militia, the Roman military became a highly organized force that expanded Roman rule from Britain to North Africa and from Spain to Mesopotamia, helping shape one of the biggest empires in history.

Despite many changes in the structure of Roman leadership, the army remained a symbol of Rome's enduring strength. Throughout civil wars, foreign invasions, and even peacetime, it evolved, mirroring the society it served. Far-reaching campaigns across Europe, in Asia Minor, and across northern Africa influenced the development of siege techniques and engineering expertise, leading to the construction of sturdy, high-quality roads, many of which laid the groundwork for future transportation routes that remain in use today. Influential figures such as Gaius Marius, Sulla, Pompey, Julius Caesar, and Octavian Augustus shaped it into one of history's most formidable military machines.

The Roman army became a melting pot of cultures and one of the ways non-Romans could become citizens. The Roman state encompassed many different regions, cultures, and languages, and the army provided a way to unify these peoples. The strongest point of the Roman state was its culture, orderliness, and focus on infrastructure and organization, which existed, as if in a microcosm, in the form of the Roman military for centuries before the Roman state expanded to three continents.

Most of the biggest battles of classical antiquity were associated with the Roman army, one way or another. However, no army is immune to decline. Internal disharmony, economic pressures, corruption, and relentless invasions by Germanic tribes, the Huns, and the Persians eventually weakened and dismantled the Roman military in the West over several centuries. For more than two thousand years, the army underwent significant transformations in size, organization, equipment, and tactics. In this book, our focus will be on the development of the Roman army until the collapse of the Western Roman Empire in 476 CE. The division of the Roman Empire marked the end of an era, although the Eastern Roman Empire (the Byzantine Empire) preserved many ancient Roman military traditions for centuries to come.

This book will also show how the Roman military really functioned. In movies, TV shows, and video games, we mainly see the glorious, exciting side of the Roman military, and you will certainly experience this in the book. But we want to go further; we want to showcase the other, perhaps less exciting but equally interesting side of Roman military history. For every great day and great battle, there were countless days, months, and years of digging trenches, pitching camps, holding guard, besieging a town, and countless small skirmishes. Today, there are so many routine activities in the day-to-day life of a soldier, and it was not much different in ancient Roman times. The activities, of course, changed, but the training, long waiting, and night watches remained.

Join us on our journey through time, starting from the earliest days of the Roman military. We will voyage across centuries of military development and exciting events, stopping to catch our breath with the resting Roman armies, pitching camp for the night, and awaiting the next day's orders from generals. Our journey will end with the fall of the Western Roman Empire.

Chapter 1: The Birth of the Roman Legion

Ancient Rome's armed forces stand as one of the most effective and long-lived military institutions in recorded history. Their influence on tactics, organization, and military thinking stretched well beyond the empire's collapse. The army's main responsibilities were expansion, defending the frontier, and keeping the peace across a territory that at its height covered more than 5.9 million square kilometers (2.3 million square miles).

Rome was traditionally founded in 753 BCE. Traces of settlement in the region go back further, to the beginning of the last millennium BCE, though what exactly existed there before is difficult to say. Early Roman warfare was nothing like organized conflict. There were small raids, the occasional ritualized battle, and skirmishes that mattered more for reputation than territory. The "armies" of this period were likely small warrior bands formed around aristocratic leaders, their kin, and dependents. Glory was personal. A leader proved himself through fighting, gathered followers because of it, and built his power from the ground up.

Trying to assess the accuracy of any of this is a challenge. Romans didn't start writing their own history until the late 3rd century BCE. Everything before the Roman Republic (before 509 BCE) sits in a haze somewhere between legend and fact. Most of it is probably myth.

Romulus, Rome's first king, moved quickly to stabilize the city after its founding. There was one huge problem: there weren't enough women. A city without women would not last past a generation. Neighboring communities refused to allow marriages with Romans, closing off the usual route to alliance-building. Negotiations went nowhere.

What followed was not subtle. Early in Rome's history, Romulus is said to have organized a festival of games. This invitation was extended to neighboring peoples, including Caenina, Crustumerium, and Antemnae, along with the Sabines from Sabinum. During the festival, the Romans seized the Sabine women and drove off the men. The kings of Caenina, Crustumerium, and Antemnae invaded. Rome fought back and won each engagement.

The first to fall was Caenina and its king, Acron. Romulus marked the victory with a ceremony that Roman tradition later described as the first Roman triumph. Historians treat the whole account as legendary, with the first actual triumph belonging to the Republican period. A triumph was a ceremonial procession through the city in which the victorious commander paraded captured spoils and prisoners through Rome before making sacrifices to the gods. It would be authorized by the Senate.

After the victory, Romulus dedicated a temple to Jupiter Feretrius, the aspect of the god associated with the spoils of war. Then the Sabines themselves declared war. Battles followed. And then something unexpected happened. The Sabine women, who were now married to Romans, stopped the fighting. Livy recorded their words: "If it is kinship, if it is marriage that you cannot bear, turn your wrath against us; we are the cause of war, wounds and death of our husbands and parents. We would rather die than live without one or the other, as widows or as orphans."[i]

That was the end of the war. According to Roman tradition, the Sabines and Romans merged into a single people, ruled jointly by Titus Tatius of the Sabines and Romulus. The episode is known as either "the rape of the Sabine women" or "the abduction of the Sabine women." Historians still debate what it actually meant. Was it sexual violence? A myth constructed to explain marriage alliances and population growth?

---

[i] Titus Livius, *From the Founding of the City*, 2012, p.45

Both? The joint rule was short. Titus Tatius was said to have been killed after five years, and Romulus ruled alone again.

Intervention of the Sabine Women by Jacques-Louis David (1799)[1]

Romulus is credited with founding Rome's core institutions, including the Senate and the army. His successor, Numa Pompilius, governed differently. Numa Pompilius was less interested in war. He restructured the calendar, introduced formal religious holidays, and focused on law. Livy put it plainly: "Numa wanted to rebuild the new city (already built by force and weapons) with religion and laws."[i] Rome's third king, Tullus Hostilius, reversed that course and warred with the Sabines again.

The Roman legion likely developed from a hoplite-style phalanx, though the precise origins remain uncertain. The phalanx came from ancient Greece. A phalanx was a dense, tight block of infantry. They stood shoulder to shoulder, several ranks deep. Hoplites carried helmets, greaves, and shields. They fought as a unit. Cohesion mattered far more than individual skill; a man who broke formation endangered everyone around him. Early Roman armies seem to have fought this way.

---

[i] Mesihović, Salmedin, *Orbis Romanvs,* University of Sarajevo, 2015, p.165

What emerged over time was something different. The manipular legion used a checkerboard formation (the quincunx) rather than a single unbroken line. Units were spaced apart, with the gaps in one line backed by units in the line behind. Three lines of infantry made up the legion. Hastati, typically the youngest soldiers, held the front. Behind them were the principes, more experienced fighters ready to push forward if the first line buckled. At the rear stood the triarii, veterans held back for the worst moments. They were committed only when things were genuinely desperate.

Each line was divided into maniples. The checkerboard pattern meant exhausted frontline soldiers could fall back through the gaps while fresh troops moved up to replace them. It also meant the formation could hold together on uneven ground, where a rigid phalanx had a tendency to fracture.

According to Livy, an early Roman legion consisted of three thousand infantry and three hundred horsemen, drawn equally from Rome's three founding tribes: the Ramnes, Tities, and Luceres.[i] Each corps of a thousand men was broken down further into ten groups of centuries, corresponding to the ten curiae of each tribe.[ii]

The three founding tribes eventually lost their importance and were replaced by a territorial system. Under reforms traditionally attributed to Servius Tullius, Rome was divided into twenty-one tribes. Four were city tribes (*tribus urbanae*)—Suburana, Esquilina, Collina, and Palatina—each named for a district of Rome. The other seventeen covered the rural countryside.

The three kings who followed Numa—Tullus Hostilius, Ancus Marcius, and Lucius Tarquinius Priscus—were remembered as warriors. Tradition credits them with campaigns against Alba Longa, the Sabines, and the Etruscan city of Veii. Tarquinius Priscus expanded the Senate by a hundred members. He also tried to reform the cavalry by creating new units outside the old tribal structure, but the augur (priest) Attus Navius blocked it. They compromised. Tarquinius Priscus would double the existing units rather than create new ones. He later celebrated victories over the Sabines and neighboring tribes.

---

[i] The Ramnes were named after Romulus. Tities was named after Titus. The origins of Luceres remain unknown.

[ii] A curia is a clan-based political unit.

On the cultural side, a victory over Apiolae gave the Romans occasion to establish the grounds for a circus, later the Circus Maximus. The games became one of the most enduring legacies of Roman life.

Two principal sources cover this period: Livy and Dionysius of Halicarnassus. Both attribute a major overhaul of Rome's political, military, and social organization to Servius Tullius, who ruled from 579 to 534 BCE. Servius doubled the number of soldiers and reorganized them by wealth. By the close of the 5th century, the army had grown to somewhere between five thousand and six thousand men, divided into centuries of up to one hundred soldiers each. Citizens were divided by age as well. Iuniores (juniors), men aged seventeen to forty-six, served in the field army, while seniores (seniors), aged forty-seven to sixty, generally handled local defense.

Each class equipped itself according to its means. The equestrians (*equites*), the wealthiest, served as cavalry. The first class of the wealthiest citizens served as heavy infantry. They had swords, long spears, and equipment resembling that of a hoplite. The second class carried similar arms but with lighter and less expensive equipment. The third and fourth classes went lighter still, armed with javelins. The fifth class, the poorest men still wealthy enough to count, likely served as skirmishers, using slings and stones.

This was the foundation of the Comitia Centuriata (Centuriate Assembly), the assembly at which the Roman people voted to declare war. Military service wasn't just a duty. It was a marker of citizenship and proof of one's standing. The five classes translated directly into centuries within the legion, binding political participation to military obligation in a way that defined what it meant to be Roman.

Anatomy of the Roman Legion

To understand the Roman army, you have to stop treating it as a single thing. It wasn't. What Servius Tullius organized in the 6th century BCE looked almost nothing like the army that fought at Cannae in 216 BCE, and neither of these armies resembles the imperial legion that held the Rhine frontier under Augustus. The Roman military evolved constantly, sometimes gradually, sometimes in response to a catastrophic defeat. Putting those three very different systems into one description produces a muddy picture.

The Servian Army (6th century BCE)

Servius reorganized Rome's military around property classes, which we covered above. The army of this period was essentially a levy of citizen infantry, organized into centuries and drawn up in a Greek-style hoplite formation. It was not even organized into cohorts; that happened much later.

The Manipular Legion (roughly 4th–2nd centuries BCE)

The real break came during the Samnite Wars, which we will cover in more detail in the next chapter. The exact timing is hard to pin down, as the shift from phalanx to manipular system was gradual rather than happening all at once. The terrain of Samnium was rugged and broken, making it poorly suited for the rigid phalanx formation that the Romans and their Latin and Etruscan contemporaries still relied on. A series of defeats, the worst of which was the humiliation at the Caudine Forks, forced the Romans to rethink their military structure.

What replaced the phalanx was more flexible. It is sometimes described as "a phalanx with joints." The key unit was no longer the phalanx but the maniple (*manipulus*). A maniple of hastati or principes typically contained around 120 men arranged in three ranks of 40 during combat. Triarii maniples were half that, about 60 men.

The first detailed account of how this worked comes from Polybius, who wrote in the mid-2nd century BCE. The manipular legion was arranged in three lines. At the front were the velites, light infantry, who engaged the enemy at the opening of a battle and worked closely with the cavalry. Behind them came the hastati, the youngest and least experienced heavy infantry, who formed the first real line of battle. The principes, more seasoned soldiers, held the second line in support. At the rear stood the triarii, the veterans, who only entered the battle when things had gone badly wrong.

According to Polybius, a standard legion comprised 10 maniples of 120 hastati, 10 maniples of 120 principes, and 10 half-strength maniples of triarii at 60 men each. Add 1,200 velites and 300 cavalry, and the total came to around 4,500 soldiers. Under serious pressure, this could be stretched to 5,000.

The Early Imperial Legion

By the early imperial period, the manipular system had given way to the cohort as the primary tactical unit. Ten cohorts made up a legion. Nine of them were standard formations of six centuries each, with a century normally containing around eighty men. The first cohort was larger and more prestigious than the others. It probably consisted of five double-strength centuries, though its exact strength is debated and likely varied.

Within each century, soldiers were grouped into *contubernia*, eight men who shared a tent or barracks room. This was the smallest unit of the army. Cavalry support in this period came mainly from auxiliary units rather than from a cavalry arm within the legion itself.

The legion's eagle standard, the aquila, was one of its most sacred symbols and was closely associated with the first cohort and its senior officers. Losing it was considered the gravest dishonor a legion could suffer. This shame could define the unit's reputation for generations.

Legion Command

The imperial legion was commanded by a legate (*legatus legionis*), usually a senator of praetorian rank. Six staff officers assisted him: a senior military tribune (*tribunus laticlavius*), also of senatorial rank and the legate's second in command, plus five equestrian tribunes (*tribuni angusticlavii*). The senior professional soldier was the camp prefect (*praefectus castrorum*). He was responsible for the fortress, its logistics, and the training of the men. In the absence of the legate, command could fall to him or to the senior tribune, depending on the situation.

Below the officers were fifty-nine centurions, each commanding a century. The five centurions of the first cohort outranked all the others. At the top of that hierarchy sat the primus pilus (literally "first spear"), who commanded the first century of the first cohort. It was the peak of an enlisted career and came with a lot of authority.

Roles Within the Century

Each century had an internal structure. The optio was the centurion's appointed deputy. He stood at the rear of the formation to keep the ranks in order. The tesserarius handled the guard roster and watch passwords. The signifer carried the centurial standard, a spear shaft hung with medallions and usually topped with an open hand, representing the oath of loyalty. In battle, soldiers kept their eyes on the standard. The signifier also managed the men's pay and savings. The cornicen, the horn blower, signaled commands.

The aquilifer carried the legion's eagle, which was different from the centurial standard. This was one of the most prestigious posts in the army. The job was given to a steady, experienced soldier who understood the tactical situation well enough to keep the eagle safe under any circumstances. The imaginifer carried an image of the emperor as a reminder of where the legion's loyalty ultimately lay. Detachments from a unit also carried their own banner, called a vexillum, that displayed their name and insignia.

Centurions were professional soldiers who had risen through the ranks. In the field, they were easy to identify. They had a transverse crest on their helmet and wore mail or scale armor and shin guards. They wore the gladius, a short stabbing sword, on the left side and the pugio, a military dagger, on the right (the reverse of an ordinary legionary), and carried a vine stick (*vitis*) as both a badge of rank and a tool for enforcing discipline. Those who had distinguished themselves might also wear phalerae, decorative medals of valor. A promotion to centurion came through demonstrated ability and appointment by senior commanders, and the pay reflected the responsibility. A centurion would be paid several times the wage of an ordinary legionary, with the exact figure depending on one's rank and the period in which they served.

The legion was largely self-sufficient. Among its men were engineers, surveyors, clerks, craftsmen, and other specialists. Many of these were classed as immunes, men excused from certain camp duties because of their skills. This arrangement kept the legion functioning as more than just a fighting force. The legion built forts wherever the threat of uprising made a permanent garrison worthwhile. The layout was standardized enough that a soldier transferred from one end of the empire to the other would recognize the plan immediately. It mirrored the layout of a Roman town with additional military buildings.

Each legion carried a number and a name. For instance, there was Legio X Gemina (the Tenth "Twin" Legion). A legion could accumulate honorifics like *pia fidelis* (dutiful and loyal) for distinguished service. Over the long history of the Roman state, legions were formed, disbanded, renumbered, and renamed. Many numbers appear more than once. What each legion kept was its own identity, history, and official titles.

Recruitment and Training

The Roman army of the imperial period was a professional force. Equipment was largely standardized and supplied. Soldiers did not generally purchase their own arms and armor, as citizen-soldiers in the early Roman Republic had done.

Recruitment drew free men from across the empire, which made for a remarkably diverse force. Soldiers posted far from home served alongside men from cultures they had never encountered. Requirements shifted over time and varied by unit, but the army's expectations were broadly consistent. One had to be physically fit, in the right age range (generally young adults), and have evidence of decent character.

According to Vegetius, who wrote in the late 4th century CE and drew heavily on earlier sources, training began not with weapons but with marching. The reasoning was that a formation is only as fast as its slowest man, and a unit that cannot march in step cannot fight in step. Recruits first had to complete 20 Roman miles (about 29.6 kilometers) in five summer hours at "military pace," carrying roughly 20.5 kilograms of kit.[i] After that came the "full pace"—24 Roman miles (about 35.5 kilometers) in the same time with the same load. Gymnastics and swimming rounded out their physical conditioning.

Weapons training followed. Vegetius says instructors were often rewarded with extra rations, which shows how seriously the army took this. Legionaries trained to thrust with the gladius while sheltering behind a large rectangular shield called a scutum. Early drills used wooden gladii and pila (a heavy javelin) against a wooden post called a quintain. The training weapons were deliberately heavier than the real thing so that the actual weapons would feel light by comparison. Later came armatura, one-on-one sparring with weapons matching the real weight; this was the same training regimen used for gladiators. Roofed halls allowed these drills to continue through winter.

Beyond individual weapons work, soldiers had to learn formation drills, such as the horn calls for attack and retreat, the role of the standards as rally points, and the different march tempos. The heavy infantry had to hold its formation under pressure, grinding forward in tight order. None of it worked unless soldiers could do it automatically, without thinking. That required repetition. The same movements were drilled over and over again until they became instinct.

Upon completion of training, the new soldier swore an oath of loyalty to the Senate and Roman people in the Republican period and to the emperor during the empire.

---

[i] Summer hours are the longer daylight hours used in Roman timekeeping.

Service terms varied. Legionaries typically served around twenty years, with additional reserve obligations. Auxiliaries, who often served in roles that complemented the legions, including cavalry, archery, and light infantry, generally served twenty-five years. Upon honorable discharge, auxiliaries received Roman citizenship. Veterans could settle in a colony (*colonia*) with fellow soldiers or return home. Military diplomas, bronze documents recording the grant of citizenship and discharge rights, were issued to auxiliaries upon discharge.

The Siege of Veii (406–396 BCE)

Veii was one of the most powerful cities in the Etruscan world, sitting close enough to Rome that the two had been competing for generations. As Roman power grew through the 5th century, the Romans moved to eliminate the threat permanently. Rather than risk a direct assault on Veii's strong walls, they committed to a siege that lasted nearly a decade.

Roman tradition says Marcus Furius Camillus, a Roman general and statesman of the early Roman Republic, encircled the city, cut its supply lines, and pressed the siege until Veii finally fell. Roman engineers dug tunnels and used battering rams against the walls. Eventually, they broke through the walls and the tunnels beneath them. The fall of Veii marked a major blow to Etruscan power in central Italy.

Marcus Furius Camillus by Guillaume Rouille (1553)[2]

Camillus earned the title "second founder of Rome" for his role in the victory. The campaign also marked the first time Romans paid their citizen soldiers, which was necessary in a siege that dragged on long enough to prevent men from returning to farm their land.

The Gallic Sack

The triumph over Veii was barely settled before central Italy faced a new threat. The Gauls swept south and besieged the Etruscan city of Clusium. When Rome sent envoys to negotiate, Roman tradition claimed the envoys became involved in the fighting instead of remaining neutral. The result was a disaster. The Gauls pushed deep into Roman territory, sacked much of the city, and advanced on Capitoline Hill under cover of darkness, threatening to take the last Roman stronghold.

According to Livy, what stopped them was geese. The sacred geese of Juno, kept at the temple on Capitoline Hill, heard the Gauls climbing the rocks in the night and raised the alarm. The sentinels and dogs had missed it, but the geese didn't. Marcus Manlius, a former consul, was woken by the noise, raised the men, and beat back the Gauls who had nearly reached the top. The sentinel who slept through it was executed. Manlius was honored. The Romans did not touch the geese even during the worst of the siege, when food was at its scarcest.

The ancient sources do not agree whether Camillus arrived dramatically to defeat the Gauls in battle, as the more patriotic version of the story tells it, or whether the Romans paid a ransom. The famous scene in which the Gallic leader Brennus threw his sword onto the scales and declared "Woe to the vanquished" appears in Livy, but the heroic rescue by Camillus is widely considered a later addition. What is clear is that the Gauls eventually withdrew, and Camillus, who was appointed dictator in the aftermath, oversaw the city's reconstruction. He left Rome with a second title, "second father of the city," and in some accounts, simply "Romulus."

This episode, legendary or not, left a mark on how the Romans thought about military discipline. The failure of the night watch had nearly cost them everything.

Chapter 2: Conquest of Italy: From City-State to Hegemony

Roman expansion in Italy was not a single campaign or a clean strategic vision; it was two centuries of grinding conflict, opportunistic alliances, and hard lessons that came with defeat. The process transformed Rome from a small city-state on the Tiber into the dominant power on the Italian Peninsula.

The Roman Republic itself was founded in 509 BCE, following the overthrow of King Tarquinius Superbus. The following century brought serious wars with the Etruscans. In 390 BCE, a Gallic invasion from the north nearly destroyed the city entirely. Then came the Samnites, a powerful tribal confederation from the Apennines, who would test Rome repeatedly in three separate wars. When that was finally resolved, Rome faced its last major challenge to supremacy in the Pyrrhic War in the early 3rd century BCE. Throughout it all, Rome expanded through a combination of conquest and incorporation, granting rights or full citizenship to various Italic peoples, tying them into a growing system increasingly centered on the Senate.

At the start of the Roman Republic, the dominant forces in Italy were the Etruscan cities to the north. Rome's influence among the Latin cities was limited. As Etruscan power gradually declined, it opened space for other forces, Rome among them, to assert themselves. The first known conflict between Rome and the Latin cities came at the turn of the 6th to the 5th century BCE. As Rome pushed to consolidate regional power, the Latin cities unified against the common threat, forming what became known as the Latin League. This alliance lasted for several centuries, drawing in various villages and tribes as time passed.

The war between the Romans and Latins lasted several years before ending with Rome's victory at the Battle of Lake Regillus in 496 BCE. The battle strengthened Roman influence in Latium (central western Italy), though it did not settle the question of dominance permanently; that would come later, after the Latin War of 340–338 BCE. Following the battle, a few minor skirmishes occurred before a peace treaty was established.

Dionysius of Halicarnassus records its terms: "Let there be peace between the Romans and all the Latin cities as long as the heavens and the earth shall remain where they are. Neither let them make war upon one another, nor bring in foreign enemies, nor grant safe passage to those who shall make war upon either. Let them assist one another, when warred upon, with all their forces, and let each have an equal share of the spoils and booty taken in their common wars."[i] Despite this, resentment simmered. Some Latin cities never fully accepted Rome's growing influence.

The Samnites were a formidable presence. They were a powerful tribal confederation from the Apennine highlands. They had their eyes set on the territory adjacent to Rome. The First Samnite War, traditionally dated to 343–341 BCE, began over Campania. The city of Capua and its surrounding region had appealed to Rome for protection as Samnite pressure increased, and Rome answered. The battles at Mount Gaurus and at Suessula in 343 BCE followed. Prominent Roman commanders in this early part of the war included the consul Marcus Valerius Corvinus and the war tribune Publius Decius Mus.

The Romans held their own against the Samnites, but the situation became complicated when many Latin allies began to revolt. Around 340 BCE, Rome found itself managing two threats at the same time. The battle at the Veseris River, led by consuls Publius Decius Mus and Titus Manlius Torquatus, was one of the more striking moments of the war. Publius Decius called on the pontifex maximus (the chief priest in Rome) to help him perform a ritual of *devotio*, a vow to offer his own life and those of the enemy to the gods of the underworld in exchange for victory. He then rode into the thick of battle and died. Rome won.

---

[i] Dionysius of Halicarnassus, *Roman Antiquities*, Book IV: Chapter 95, Loeb Classical Library, 1940.

There was a related ritual, *evocatio*, which worked differently. A Roman commander would call upon the enemy's own patron deity to abandon them and transfer allegiance to Rome, promising better maintenance of the cult in return. Both rituals reflect how deeply Roman commanders fused religious obligation with military command.

The disorder of the First Samnite War gave the Latin cities an opening. They sent Rome an ultimatum demanding the restoration of the previous situation between them and Rome. Rome refused. Remarkably, the Samnites, Rome's recent enemies, sided with Rome against the Latins. The Roman and Samnite forces crossed the territory of the Aequi, descended through the Apennines into Campania, and defeated the combined Latin and Campanian armies near Suessa Aurunca. The Romans then pushed through, defeating the Latins along with their Volscian and Campanian allies. By 338 BCE, the Romans had imposed their own terms.

The settlement was decisive. The cities closest to Rome were absorbed outright, and their residents were granted Roman citizenship with full rights, including *ius commercii* (the right to trade and own property) and *ius connubii* (the right to marry Romans). Only Tibur and Praeneste retained a measure of autonomy; they were treated as allies rather than subjects.

This general settlement had consequences far beyond the immediate moment. It established the framework of a confederation designed to eventually encompass all of Italy. Rome's allies supplied troops and served alongside Roman forces in shared campaigns but paid no tribute. That arrangement generated a genuine, if unequal, sense of common interest.

Before Rome could press further, it had to deal with the Samnites again. The Second Samnite War broke out in 327 BCE, sparked primarily by the contest over Neapolis (Naples). Rome's allies, the Capuans, had moved against the city, which was receiving Samnite support. Both sides found themselves drawn in through their respective obligations. The war started in Rome's favor, but the Samnite highlands were punishing terrain for Roman formations, and their momentum stalled. Neither side could break through the other's lines.

A turning point came in 325 BCE when Roman forces reached the Adriatic coast for the first time. However, a direct assault on Samnium itself brought the offensive to a halt. And in 321 BCE came a catastrophe. A Roman force of perhaps twenty thousand men was trapped at the Caudine Forks (the Furculae Caudinae) and forced to surrender. The defeated soldiers were made to pass under a yoke of spears, wearing only their tunics. The yoke, called the *iugum*, was an ancient warrior ceremony repurposed here as deliberate humiliation; it was like a symbolic stripping of the soldiers' warrior status. Most of the men were released afterward, but supposedly six hundred hostages were left behind.

Medallion depicting the Romans going under the yoke[8]

For the Romans, this was not the end. After years of rebuilding, they went back on the offensive. The war dragged on for more than a decade as both sides fought for control of central Italy. By the early 300s BCE, Rome had regained the initiative, capturing Bovianum, a key Samnite city, around 305 BCE and pressing on to take places such as Fregellae, Calatia, and Nola. The struggle finally ended with a peace treaty in 304 BCE. The agreement did not destroy Samnite independence, but it forced them to recognize the growing power of Rome.

The peace did not hold. In 299 BCE, the Gauls and Etruscans invaded Roman territory. A potential Samnite alliance with these forces threatened to undo everything Rome had built. The Third Samnite War began in 298 BCE. Rome responded by advancing into Etruscan territory while those forces were occupied elsewhere, effectively neutralizing them.

The decisive engagement came at Sentinum in 295 BCE. Rome committed four legions. One of the consuls, Publius Decius Mus, performed a devotio before the battle; this was the same ritual his father had performed at Veseris half a century earlier. Rome won. The Etruscans negotiated peace, and the Samnites were crushed.

What remained of Samnite territory was absorbed or reorganized. Most came under Roman control, and the rest of the lands were incorporated as *civitas sine suffragio*, cities without voting rights. They were subject to Rome's authority without representation in its assemblies. Central Italy was now Roman. In 283 BCE, Rome repelled a Gallic incursion at Lake Vadimo, effectively closing the chapter on major internal Italian resistance.

Two figures from the Third Samnite War are worth talking about. Manius Curius Dentatus, the general who ultimately broke Samnite resistance, was a *homo novus*, a man without aristocratic lineage who had risen through ability and popular support rather than family connections. Later Roman accounts speak of how he embodied Republican virtues. He took only a modest plot of land, farmed it himself, and refused personal enrichment. His biography became a template for generations. The other notable commander was Lucius Cornelius Scipio Barbatus, whose tombstone Livy mentions as the earliest Roman inscription naming a historical figure.

After the Samnites, Rome's expansion brought it into contact with the Greek colonies of southern Italy. The most powerful was Tarentum, a Spartan colony and a major Mediterranean city. Tensions with Rome dated to 282 BCE, when a Roman fleet entered waters near Tarentum in violation of an earlier treaty. The citizens of Tarentum attacked the Roman ships and insulted the envoys Rome sent in response. Rome dispatched a consul to negotiate. The Tarentines responded by calling in outside help. This help was none other than Pyrrhus, King of Epirus.

Pyrrhus was an ambitious man in a complicated position. He had designs on the Macedonian throne but no firm grip on it. The invitation from Tarentum offered him a chance to strengthen his standing. In 280 BCE, he arrived in Italy with around twenty-two thousand soldiers, three thousand cavalry, and approximately twenty war elephants. The Romans sent a force under Consul Valerius Levinus. The armies met near Heraclea, on the Siris River in 280 BCE. Rome lost. Several tribes, including the Samnites, shifted allegiance to Pyrrhus.

Pyrrhus of Epirus⁴

The second battle came at Asculum in Apulia in 279 BCE. Two brutal days of fighting left the Romans with around six thousand dead. Pyrrhus lost roughly half that. He had technically won, but the cost rattled him. He reportedly responded, "Another such victory and we are lost." That is where the phrase "Pyrrhic victory" comes from. It was not the tactical outcome alone, but more so Pyrrhus's own recognition that winning at this rate was indistinguishable from losing. His army was smaller to begin with. He could not replace men the way Rome could. He sent terms saying Rome should dissolve its Italian alliances and leave the Greek cities of the south alone. Rome declined.

Around this time, the Galatians had invaded Macedonia and Greece, another crisis that complicated Pyrrhus's long-term ambitions since he still coveted the Macedonian throne. Carthage, watching Pyrrhus's campaigns with concern about its own interests in Sicily, made a pact with Rome. Neither side would negotiate a separate peace with the Greeks.

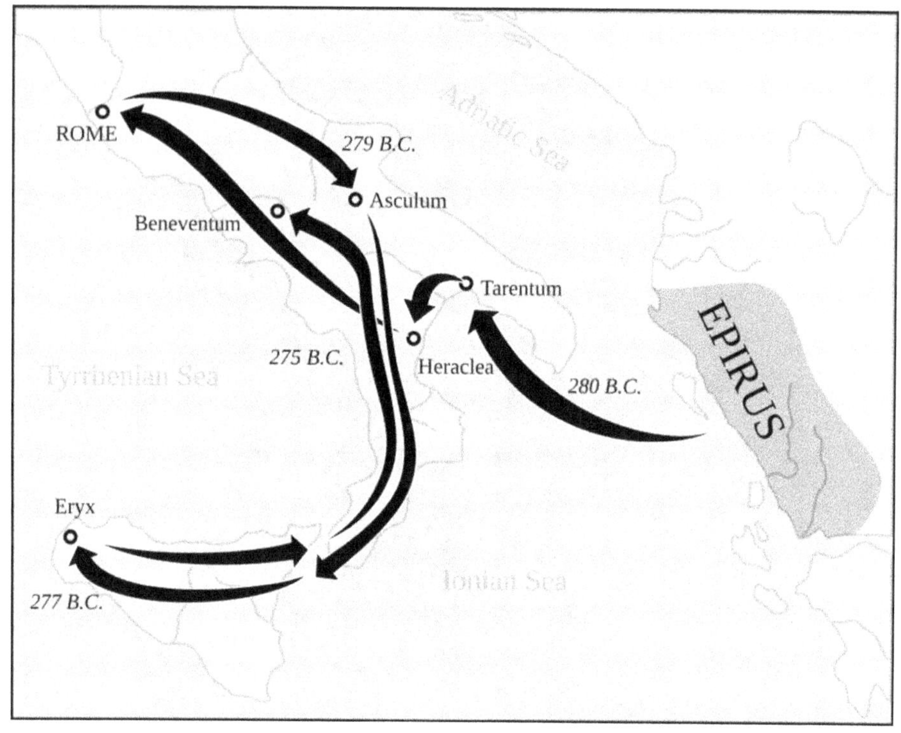

Battle sites of the Pyrrhic War[5]

One episode from this period has stuck in historical memory, repeated for centuries as an example of Roman character. A consul named Gaius Fabricius was sent to negotiate prisoner exchanges with Pyrrhus. The king, having heard of Fabricius's reputation for integrity, tried to buy him. He offered lavish gifts, which Fabricius rejected. At a later meeting, Pyrrhus arranged for an elephant to rear up behind Fabricius during negotiations, apparently hoping to unsettle him.

Fabricius didn't even flinch. "Just as I was not swayed by your wealth yesterday," he said, "I am even less afraid of your elephant today."[i] Pyrrhus's own physician then approached Fabricius privately and offered to poison the king for a fee. Fabricius reported the offer to Pyrrhus, who had the physician executed. He then released all Roman prisoners without conditions. Rome released its own captives in return. However, peace failed because neither Rome nor Pyrrhus was willing to compromise.

In 278 BCE, Pyrrhus shifted his focus to Sicily, capturing several cities including Palermo, Seleste, and Selinunte. He failed at Lilybaeum, which stopped his momentum and began to erode his support among the Sicilian Greeks. While he was occupied in Sicily, Rome was racking up victories over the Samnites and other Italian tribes in 278, 277, and 276 BCE. Pyrrhus finally made the tough decision to return to Italy.

The decisive engagement came at Beneventum in 275 BCE. Roman archers scattered the Greek war elephants, which turned on their own lines. Rome won. The city's name was changed from Maleventum, meaning something like "ill wind," to Beneventum, meaning "good event."[ii] Manius Curius Dentatus celebrated a triumph in Rome with four captured elephants parading through the city.

Pyrrhus left Italy in 275 BCE, leaving Tarentum under the command of a garrison. The city held its fortifications until 272 BCE, when it was forced to surrender. It gave hostages to Rome and dismantled its fleet. Among those taken to Rome in the aftermath was a Tarentine Greek named Livius Andronicus, though whether he came as a hostage or in some other capacity is debated. He went on to become one of the earliest Latin authors. Pyrrhus himself died in 272 BCE at Argos. He was killed during street fighting against the forces of Antigonus II Gonatas.

With Pyrrhus gone and Tarentum neutralized, the Samnites accepted Roman supremacy at last. Under Roman command, they helped take the Etruscan city of Volsinii in 264 BCE. That is generally regarded as the end of the conquest of Italy.

The whole process took roughly two centuries, though the military effort was far from continuous. Most of Rome's opponents were tribal

---

[i] Mesihović, Salmedin, *Orbis Romanvs*, University of Sarajevo, 2015, p.272-273

[ii] Mirković, Miroslava, *Istorija Rimske države*, Službeni glasnik, 2014, p.104

forces without unified political structures or the resources to sustain prolonged campaigns. As Rome itself changed, growing from a cluster of villages into a city with a large population and an organized state, its approach to war changed with it. What began as ritualized raids and skirmishes between aristocrats became a machine. Rome had a state-funded, state-organized professional army capable of sustained campaigns across an entire peninsula. The next stage would take that machine beyond Italy entirely, toward Sicily, Corsica, Sardinia, and the coast of North Africa.

Chapter 3: The Punic Wars: Clashes with Carthage

1st Punic War

Lands owned by Romans and Carthaginians before the First Punic War[6]

After two centuries of grinding warfare, Rome had forged an Italian confederacy and emerged as one of the most formidable powers in the Mediterranean world. Its military strength in terms of manpower, organization, and strategic depth gave it exceptional capabilities that few rivals could match.

After defeating Pyrrhus, a skilled commander who had tested Rome, the Roman Republic became a power that others wanted on their side. Egypt was the first major Hellenistic kingdom to open diplomatic relations in 273 BCE. Various Greek city-states took note of Rome's rise as well. And Carthage, the great Phoenician colonial power with deep commercial and political stakes across the western Mediterranean, watched closely because Roman foreign policy was beginning to affect Carthaginian interests.

The treaty between Rome and Carthage, first established in the 6th century, was revised in 279 BCE during the war against Pyrrhus. Once the southern Italian ports came under Roman control, the interests of Naples and Tarentum folded into Rome's orbit as well. A collision between the two powers was becoming increasingly likely. There is a tradition that says Pyrrhus, on leaving Italy, remarked that he was "leaving the battleground for Romans and Carthaginians."[i] Whether he said it or not, the observation came true.

On land, Rome was clearly the stronger force. At sea, Carthage had no serious rival. Each was backed by substantial allies. Rome was backed by the Etruscans, Samnites, Umbrians, and Italian Greeks (most of them were Roman allies or subjects by this point). Carthage was supported by the Berber and Libyan peoples from its North African territories. The collision, when it came, began in Sicily.

The trigger was the Mamertines, Campanian mercenaries who had seized the city of Messana around 288 BCE and established themselves there by force. Hiero II, ruler of Syracuse and the only significant independent power left on the island, raised an army to deal with them. The Mamertines were divided. Some wanted to appeal to Rome. Others preferred Carthage, which had the fleet to reach them quickly and already maintained ports in Sardinia, Corsica, and southern Iberia. Rome understood what was at stake. Carthaginian control of Messana would put a major hostile naval power just across the water from the Italian coast.

The Roman Senate could not agree on what to do, so the decision was pushed to the citizen assembly, the Comitia Centuriata, which was persuaded by the prospect of plunder and new territory. Appius Claudius Caudex was appointed consul and sent with a force to

[i] Mirković, Miroslava, *Istorija Rimske države*, Službeni glasnik, 2014, p.123

Messana. The Mamertines requested that he take control of the city. Carthage, meanwhile, allied with Hiero to defend Syracuse. That friction ignited the First Punic War in 264 BCE.

Two years in, after negotiations went nowhere, the Romans laid siege to Agrigentum, the Greek colony known as Akragas, one of Carthage's key strongholds on the island. The siege dragged on for six months. Carthage sent a relief force under Hanno, reportedly comprising fifty thousand infantry, six thousand cavalry, and sixty war elephants. The Romans, fielding a force that ancient sources put at a substantial size, drove Hanno back and eventually took the city. It was a serious blow.

Losing Agrigentum pushed Carthage toward its natural advantage: the sea. While Carthage pressed Rome's coastal positions with its fleet, the Romans scrambled to build one of their own. Until this point, their naval forces had consisted mainly of ships contributed by allies like Tarentum, Elea, and Neapolis (the *socii navales*). Rome had no real tradition of naval warfare. What it built was a solution to that problem.

Unfamiliar with open-water tactics, the Romans leaned into what they knew: close combat. Their ships were fitted with a boarding device called the corvus, a spiked gangplank that could be dropped onto an enemy deck, locking the ships together and turning a sea battle into something resembling a land engagement. The first test, at the Lipari Islands, went badly. But at Mylae in 260 BCE, under Consul Gaius Duilius, Rome won its first real naval victory. Duilius celebrated with a triumph in Rome and was honored with a columna rostrata, a column decorated with the prows of captured enemy ships.

Roman corvus naval boarding device[7]

Emboldened, Rome went further. A fleet of 330 ships was assembled and sent toward Africa. The commanders were Consuls Marcus Atilius Regulus and Lucius Manlius Vulso. The Carthaginian fleet was commanded by Hanno and Hamilcar. The battle that followed, at Cape Ecnomus in 256 BCE, was one of the largest naval engagements in ancient history. Carthage brought around 350 ships. The Romans had 330, plus the corvus. The boarding device proved decisive, and Rome won. The expeditionary force, around 140,000 men in total, landed on African soil not long after.

Local Numidian tribes, themselves in conflict with Carthage, joined in attacking the city. Carthage was forced to open peace negotiations. Regulus demanded, among other things, the surrender of the Carthaginian fleet and the payment of a massive tribute. These terms were so harsh that Carthage had no real choice but to fight on. They brought in a Spartan mercenary commander, Xanthippus of Lacedaemon, who reorganized the Carthaginian army and used their elephants and cavalry to devastating effect in open terrain. The Romans were routed, and Regulus was captured.

A new Roman fleet was sent to evacuate the survivors. It succeeded, but on the return voyage, the fleet was caught in a catastrophic storm off Sicily and almost entirely destroyed. The disaster wiped out most of the men and ships Rome had committed to the African campaign.

Despite that catastrophe, the war ground on for another fifteen years. Rome won battles across Sicily, cutting Carthaginian supply lines and steadily tightening control. It ended in 241 BCE at the Battle of the Aegates Islands, where Rome destroyed the Carthaginian fleet and forced a peace settlement. Sicily became Rome's first overseas territory.

The victory came at a steep price. Rome had lost enormous numbers of men and multiple fleets, many of them to storms. Coastal regions had been raided and devastated. However, Carthage had suffered worse. Its military was largely mercenary, and paying those men after a string of defeats strained its finances to the breaking point. Rebellions broke out in Libya and Sardinia. Hamilcar Barca (not the same Hamilcar at the Battle of Cape Ecnomus) and Hanno eventually suppressed them, but the effort depleted what little of Carthaginian resilience remained. Rome had won, but just barely. It had been expensive, and the Romans had no illusions about how close it had been.

2nd Punic War

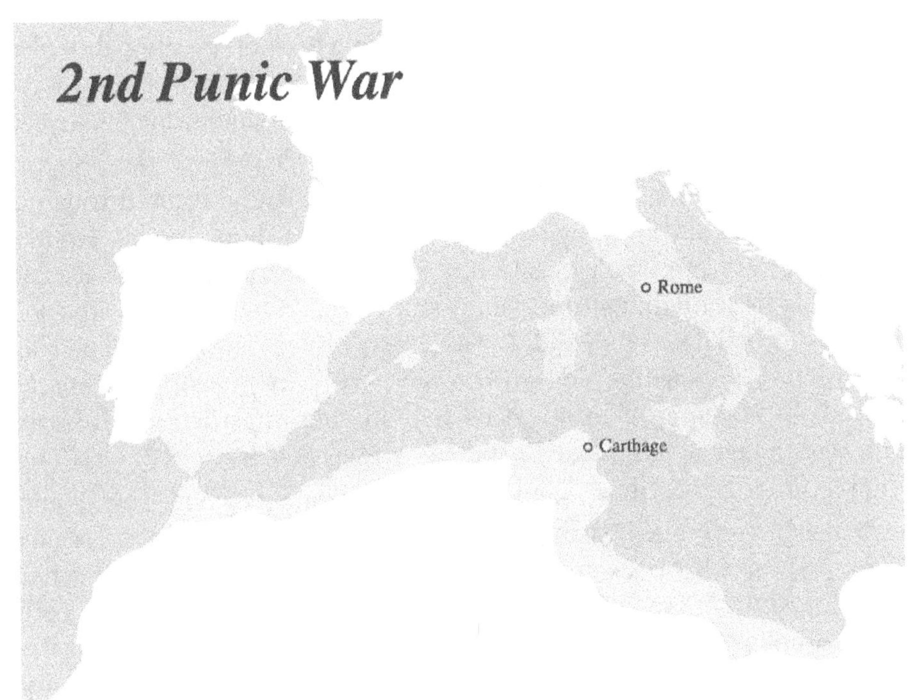

Lands owned by the Romans and Carthaginians before the Second Punic War[8]

Shortly after suppressing the mercenary rebellions, Hamilcar shifted his focus to Spain. The Iberian Peninsula was rich in silver, manpower, and land, and Hamilcar used all of it to rebuild Carthaginian strength from the ground up. He died in 228 BCE, and his son-in-law, Hasdrubal, took over. Hasdrubal's command was cut short, as he was assassinated in 221 BCE. Hamilcar's twenty-six-year-old son Hannibal was chosen to replace him.

The Second Punic War did not begin simply with Hannibal's rise to command. It was triggered in 219 BCE when Hannibal besieged Saguntum, a city that Rome considered under its protection. Rome demanded that Carthage surrender Hannibal, but Carthage refused. The war began formally in 218 BCE. What followed was one of the most daring campaigns in ancient history, not because Hannibal fought Rome on Roman terms but because he refused to.

The Romans' plan was to bring the war to Carthage so the fighting would be far from Italy. Hannibal anticipated this and moved first. He crossed the Pyrenees, pushed through southern Gaul, and then did something that still defies easy explanation: he crossed the Alps in late autumn of 218 BCE with tens of thousands of soldiers, cavalry, and war elephants. His army had been assembled largely in Spain, though it also included Libyan heavy troops and Numidian cavalry. These men were suited to open terrain and warm climates, not mountain passes in late October.

The losses during the crossing were severe. That he came through at all was extraordinary. Since this is primarily a book about Roman military history, we won't dwell on the mechanics of the crossing itself, but it tells us something important about Rome. The Romans expected enemies to behave as they did, to settle into winter camps, rest, and wait for spring. Campaigning slowed in winter, but it rarely stopped entirely. Hannibal's appearance in northern Italy in autumn, when the Romans expected the usual lull, caused panic.

Hannibal spent the march building alliances where he could, particularly with Gallic tribes who had their own grievances against Rome. These alliances were never guaranteed. Some tribes resisted him outright, while many others held back and waited to see how the early battles went before committing to either side. Hannibal understood that he was operating in entirely unfamiliar territory, deep in enemy country, far from any Carthaginian base. Friendly locals meant food, intelligence, and security for his flanks. He needed all three. For much of the march, he pushed forward largely on his own, battling the resistance of natives along the route as much as the terrain itself. The conditions were punishing, and the army that descended from the Alps into northern Italy was a fraction of what had set out.

The first significant clash came at the Ticino River in 218 BCE. The Roman consul Publius Cornelius Scipio had been heading for Spain when the scale of Hannibal's advance forced him to turn back. What happened at the Ticino was not a full pitched battle; it was primarily a cavalry engagement, with both sides probing rather than committing everything they had. Ancient battles often worked this way. The two armies would shadow each other for days, generals drawing their men into formation and then standing them down again, watching the enemy's movements and waiting for ground and weather that suited them. Soldiers in those camps knew the enemy was sometimes only a few kilometers away. They were close enough to hear them and, in some cases, could see their movements. They had to live with that knowledge while the waiting dragged on.

When the engagement at the Ticino River finally came, Hannibal's cavalry proved decisive. Roman velites (light infantry) advanced and prepared to throw their javelins. The Carthaginian horsemen charged before they could release them. The velites pulled back in a hurry. Roman and Gallic cavalry moved up to counter but found their advance tangled with the retreating skirmishers; they couldn't build any momentum. Then a part of the Carthaginian cavalry swung wide and threatened not only the oncoming Roman horsemen but the small escort surrounding Scipio himself. That was the moment that broke the battle. The velites fled, and the Roman line unraveled. Scipio was badly wounded. Tradition holds he was pulled from the field by his teenage son, who bore the same name, Publius Cornelius Scipio. The Romans retreated across the river.

They fell back to Piacenza. There, Gallic allies who had been fighting alongside Rome began to waver, then broke entirely. Around two thousand of them joined Hannibal in an act of open mutiny. They had watched Scipio lose and chose who they thought would be the ultimate victor. At the Ticino River, Hannibal had committed perhaps six thousand of his roughly twenty-six thousand men. He had won with a fraction of his force, and now, he had Gallic troops joining him.

The defeat alarmed Rome enough that the Senate sent the second consul, Tiberius Sempronius Longus, north to reinforce Scipio. The Battle of the Trebia, sometime in late December 218 BCE, would be on an entirely different scale from the skirmish at the Ticino River.

The two armies took up positions on opposite banks of the Trebia. They spent days watching each other. Before the main battle, a skirmish broke out. A Carthaginian raiding party sent to plunder nearby settlements was intercepted by Roman forces and took heavy casualties. The Romans were elated. They had bloodied Hannibal's men and forced him to pull back. Longus took this as a sign that the moment had come to end the invasion with one decisive blow. It was his biggest mistake.

Hannibal had set a trap and was simply waiting for the Romans to walk into it. He had already positioned his younger brother Mago with a force of around two thousand mixed cavalry and infantry, concealed in the scrub near the riverbank, well away from the Carthaginian camp. He had ordered his own men to be fed and warmed before dawn, ensuring they were ready for battle. Early in the morning, his Numidian cavalry crossed the Trebia and began harassing the Roman camp. The Numidians were pushed back, but then they came straight back and harassed the Romans again. Longus, commanding roughly forty thousand men, including Roman legions and allied contingents, took the bait. He ordered his army across the river without waiting for breakfast and without time for the river to warm up.

Crossing the Trebia in December was brutal. On horseback, it was difficult enough. For the infantry, it was something else. The water was chest-deep in places and freezing. The men arrived on the far bank cold, wet, and hungry before a battle that was already underway. The Roman heavy infantry pushed hard in the center nonetheless, as it always did, and for a time, the Romans seemed to be getting the better of Hannibal's center. However, on the flanks, it was a different story. Carthaginian cavalry overpowered the Roman horsemen on both sides and drove them from the field, then wheeled back to hit the Roman rear. Mago's concealed force came out of hiding and struck from behind.

The Roman center was being ground down from three directions at once. The light infantry and cavalry were gone. Longus, seeing that the bulk of his force had been broken, ordered a retreat. A core of around ten thousand men, those in the tightest formation, managed to cut through the Carthaginian center and make it back to Piacenza. Most of the other men were killed or captured.

Longus returned to Rome to oversee elections for the following year's consuls. The new consuls for 217 BCE were Gaius Flaminius and Gnaeus Servilius Geminus.

Before reaching the battlefield, Hannibal had to cross the Arno marshes. The army waded through floodwater for four days and three nights. The water was up to their chests in places, and soldiers rested on the bodies of dead horses when they could find nowhere dry to stand. The losses were severe. They lost horses, men, and almost all of the remaining elephants. Only one elephant survived. Hannibal himself contracted a severe eye infection during the crossing that eventually cost him the sight in one eye. He recovered and kept moving.

Flaminius stationed his forces near Arretium to block Hannibal's route south. Hannibal bypassed him. This was a deliberate slight designed to draw Flaminius out in a hurry without giving him time to think. It worked. Flaminius commanded four legions and was burning to confront Hannibal directly. The Gallic tribes of the north were increasingly drifting toward Carthage, unsure whether Rome could stop the invasion, and Flaminius knew that every day without a fight cost Rome allies. He marched fast.

The ground near Lake Trasimene was made for an ambush. Hills rose on one side, the lake cut off any retreat on the other, and a long, narrow passage ran between them. During the night before the battle, Hannibal sent cavalry, light infantry, and heavy infantry on a night march to take positions in the hills along the lakeshore. The main camp stayed visible. The Romans were meant to see it and follow it in.

On June 21ˢᵗ, 217 BCE, Flaminius led his army into the passage. The Romans marched in column, as was standard—three parallel lines suited for movement, to be reformed into battle order once they reached the enemy. They never got that far.

When Hannibal judged that enough Romans had entered the trap, he gave the signal. The attack came simultaneously from the front, from the hills above, and from behind. The Romans were struck before they could form up, with the lake blocking any retreat to the right. It was chaos. Flaminius was killed in the fighting. Later tradition attributed his death to a Gallic nobleman named Ducarius. Roman casualties numbered around fifteen thousand killed. Several thousand more were captured in the days that followed. A portion of the army managed to escape the trap, though for most, there was no way out. Geminus, marching separately and completely unaware that the battle was even happening, sent his cavalry ahead to link up with Flaminius. They rode directly into Hannibal's forces and were wiped out. Geminus pulled his four legions back to Ariminum.

What Hannibal demonstrated in these three engagements was a consistent and ruthless pattern: provoke, lure, fix, then hit from every direction at once. At Trebia, he had goaded a larger army into a freezing river before dawn and then collapsed its flanks. At Trasimene, he had lured an entire army into a pocket with no exit and attacked before it could even form up. The Romans were not stupid or cowardly. They simply expected enemies to fight as they did, in open formation on chosen ground. Hannibal's methods were unlike anything Roman commanders had been trained to anticipate or counter.

Trasimene scared the Senate badly enough to do something it rarely did when the Roman Republic was functioning as intended. The senators wanted to appoint a dictator. Quintus Fabius Maximus was given supreme command. He was neither the first nor the last Roman to hold the office. Later, men like Sulla, Gaius Marius, Pompey, and Caesar would eventually push the institution far beyond its original purpose. Fabius was not that kind of man, though. He took the emergency powers because the situation required them, used them as the laws intended, and did not try to hold onto them longer than necessary. He was simply tasked with dealing with the Carthaginian threat.[i]

His strategy was simple, deeply unpopular, and almost certainly right. He refused to meet Hannibal in open battle. Instead, Fabius shadowed the Carthaginian army across Italy, attacking supply parties, harassing foragers, cutting access to food wherever he could, and declining battle every time Hannibal offered it. The Romans gave him a nickname for it. He became known as Cunctator (the "Delayer"), and they did not mean it kindly, at least not at first. However, Fabius had understood something that Flaminius and Longus had not. Hannibal could not replace his losses. Every skirmish that killed Carthaginians was men that Hannibal could never get back. Rome, with its deep reserves of manpower and its ability to levy new legions after even catastrophic defeats, could absorb punishment that would cripple another army. The math favored patience.

The daily reality of the campaign under Fabius was grinding and unglamorous. The army was in almost constant motion. Camps were thrown up in the evening and dismantled the next morning so the army could move again. Soldiers were placed into formation, marched toward the enemy, and then marched back without a battle having taken place, sometimes for days on end. The enemy camp was occasionally visible, sometimes close enough that the two sides could hear each other. But the order would always come to stand down. For ordinary soldiers, that kind of sustained tension without resolution was its own form of punishment.

Night watches (the *vigiliae*) were strictly enforced. The night was divided into four watches between sunset and sunrise, and soldiers rotated through them so that no one man bore the full burden. Abandoning a watch or being caught asleep at post was not a minor infraction. Offenders could be beaten to death by their own comrades, a punishment called *fustuarium*. It was carried out after a formal court martial and on the authority of appropriate officers, like consuls, praetors, or legionary commanders.

---

[i] The office of dictator, in its original form, did not have absolute power. He did have more power than the consuls, who were directly subordinate to him. Dictators could still be held accountable by the Senate and could only exert authority in areas for which they were appointed. They defended the state and organized public games, religious rituals, and many other activities.

The watches guarded against night attacks, as well as fire, theft, and the general disorder that could unravel a large force camping in the open. Keeping proper watches required reliable timekeeping. Timekeeping in the field could be managed using clepsydrae, water clocks, though in practice, the camps relied more on signals and scheduled guard rotations than on precise measurement. The principle of the clepsydra was simple enough. Water poured into a vessel with a small hole at the bottom, and the passage of time was marked by how much had drained. More sophisticated versions with mechanical elements existed and were used by civilians, but armies tended toward the more practical version.

Hannibal plundered as he moved, trying to feed his army off enemy territory and demonstrating to Rome's Italian allies that Rome could not protect them. Fabius countered with scorched-earth measures where he could, denying Hannibal food. Reportedly, he also ordered significant increases in sacrifices during this period. Crops and livestock were said to be burned in large quantities to appease the gods. Whatever the religious rationale, it reduced what Hannibal's foragers could find.

It was not a sustainable situation for Rome, as the public was impatient. Months passed. Hannibal ranged across Italy, and Fabius followed him. Nothing seemed to change in the Romans' eyes. A cavalry commander named Marcus Minucius demonstrated during a brief period when Fabius was away (he was likely in Rome for religious ceremonies) that he could at least make the Carthaginians feel pressure, challenging them on the battlefield rather than merely hovering nearby. A plebeian tribune named Metilius, who understood how to work public sentiment, pushed for Minucius to be elevated. The result was something almost without precedent. Minucius was granted powers equal to those of the dictator, effectively splitting command of the Roman army in two. Whether he was formally a co-dictator is uncertain, but in practice, he commanded half the legions.

Near Geronium in early autumn 217 BCE, with both commanders and their respective forces present, Hannibal saw his opening. He sent some of his best troops out under the cover of night to conceal themselves in hollows in the broken terrain below the Carthaginian camp, hidden from view. Then he drew his main force out in the open, inviting a response from the Roman army. Minucius took the bait. He sent his light infantry forward. They clashed with Hannibal's troops and reached a stalemate. He committed his cavalry to break the deadlock, but the cavalry began to take losses. So, he called up the heavy infantry.

The Romans were pressing up the hill when the hidden troops came out of concealment and hit them from behind and both flanks simultaneously. The Roman force came apart. They retreated in disorder. Fabius marched his legions out, and Hannibal, unwilling to face the combined Roman force, withdrew to his camp. Minucius was not formally stripped of his command, but his authority quietly folded back under Fabius's from that point forward.

Near the Aufidus River, close to the town of Cannae in Apulia, came the worst single day in Roman military history. The Battle of Cannae in 216 BCE was not merely a defeat. It was an annihilation. Tribunes, senators, and tens of thousands of soldiers died in a single afternoon. The exact figures from ancient sources vary and are likely exaggerated, but the scale of the disaster was real enough. Hannibal's double envelopment—drawing the massive Roman center forward while his flanks curved around and closed behind it—became the most studied tactical maneuver in military history. Commanders were still trying to replicate it two thousand years later.

Rome lowered the recruitment age to about seventeen and levied additional legions. In an act of genuine desperation, the Senate authorized two legions formed from slaves purchased by the state. They had been freed and armed for service, something essentially without precedent in Roman history. This allowed Rome to keep fighting. This was perhaps the most remarkable thing about Rome in the Second Punic War, and Hannibal likely understood it better than anyone. Every time he destroyed a Roman army, Rome raised another one. The Roman Republic's capacity to absorb catastrophic losses and reconstitute itself made it almost impossible to defeat in the way a conventional war could be won. Strategically, Hannibal outmaneuvered every Roman commander he faced. However, strategy alone could not end a war against an enemy that simply refused to accept defeat.

Marcus Claudius Marcellus was sent to Sicily and eventually laid siege to Syracuse. Hiero II's death and the subsequent shift of Syracuse toward Carthage led to Marcellus camping outside the city's walls. The siege lasted from around 214 to 212 BCE. It was prolonged considerably by one man: Archimedes. The mathematician, physicist, and engineer designed and built defensive systems that repeatedly stopped Roman assaults. Cranes reached over the walls to lift ships and capsize them, and artillery rained stones on approaching soldiers. These were mechanisms the Romans had never encountered and struggled to counter. Eventually, the Romans found a way in. The city fell and was thoroughly plundered. Marcellus had wanted Archimedes taken alive, as he recognized what the man was worth. One account records a Roman soldier finding Archimedes working on a math problem during the sack of the city. He ordered Archimedes to come before Marcellus. Archimedes refused, as he needed to finish what he was doing. The soldier killed him. Marcellus was furious.

While the Italian war ground on, Rome was systematically dismantling Carthaginian power in Spain. Publius Cornelius Scipio, the consul's son who had reportedly pulled his wounded father from the field at the Ticino River years before, was sent to Spain in 210 BCE. The Senate granted him imperium through a special decree, making him the first person to receive such authority without holding a magistracy.[i] In 209 BCE, he captured Cartagena (New Carthage), the primary Carthaginian base in Spain. By 206 BCE, with local tribal support, he had cleared Carthaginian forces from the entire southern Iberian Peninsula.

Back in Italy, the balance was shifting. When Capua appealed to Hannibal for help against Rome in 211 BCE, he marched his army to the very walls of Rome in a show of force that gave rise to the phrase "Hannibal ante portas" ("Hannibal is at the gates"). Rome panicked.

However, Hannibal did not assault the city. He lacked the siege equipment. He turned back south, and Capua fell to Rome. The decision not to attack, whether forced on him by circumstance or a genuine strategic choice, diminished his standing in Carthage.

Something worse happened in 207 BCE. His brother Hasdrubal Barca had crossed the Alps with a relief force, hoping to link up with Hannibal in Italy. He never made it. Hasdrubal was intercepted and killed at the Battle of the Metaurus before he could reach his brother. Rome sent Hasdrubal's severed head south to Hannibal's camp. Whatever realistic hope Hannibal had held of receiving reinforcement from Carthage largely died with his brother.

Scipio was elected consul in 205 BCE. In 204 BCE, he crossed to Africa with an invasion force. Two years later, in 202 BCE, the two greatest commanders of the war faced each other at Zama. Hannibal had

---

[i] Imperium was the legal authority granted by the Roman state to command armies.

been recalled from Italy to defend Carthage itself. That battle ended the war. Rome had won, although it came at enormous cost and took a very long time.

At Zama in 202 BCE, Hannibal made his stand. He had slightly more infantry and around eighty elephants, but the Romans held the decisive advantage in cavalry. The Numidian king, Masinissa, had switched sides and brought his experienced horsemen with him. It cost Hannibal the battle. Carthaginian casualties were far heavier, around 20,000 killed, while Roman losses were much smaller, roughly 1,500. It was Hannibal's first decisive defeat as overall commander; he had

A marble bust thought to be of Hannibal[9]

faced setbacks before, but nothing like this. Fifteen years of campaigning in Italy, army after army destroyed, and in the end, it came down to a cavalry engagement he just could not win.

Peace was concluded in 201 BCE. The terms were punishing. Carthage could keep its African territory but had to surrender everything overseas. Most of the fleet was gone. Heavy reparations were imposed. Politically, Hannibal survived the defeat better than might be expected. He went on to serve as a political leader, a suffete, in Carthage and reportedly pushed through reforms that made him enemies among the Punic aristocracy. Roman pressure eventually forced him into exile around 195 BCE. He made his way first to the court of Antiochus III of the Seleucid Empire, where he offered his services against Rome. Later accounts place him in Armenia and Crete before he eventually settled in Bithynia, near Anatolia. The Romans tracked him there too, threatening the Bithynian king to hand him over. Hannibal had no intention of being taken alive. Most ancient sources agree he committed suicide by poison rather than falling into Roman hands. The exact year is debated—somewhere between 183 and 181 BCE—but the manner of his death is consistent across the main traditions.

The fifty years between the Second and Third Punic Wars were not peaceful for Carthage. The city recovered economically, regaining considerable wealth through agriculture and trade, which only deepened Roman suspicion. Meanwhile, the Numidians flourished under Masinissa, and Rome consistently backed him in his repeated territorial clashes with Carthage. These conflicts were the main problem. When Carthage finally took up arms against the Numidians without Rome's permission, it violated the terms of its treaty, which gave Rome the opening it wanted.

By this point, Rome had accumulated enough military and political strength to act on multiple fronts simultaneously. It had already dealt with Macedonia in the eastern Mediterranean. When the Third Punic War came, it was less a war than an execution.

The man who pushed hardest for it was Marcus Porcius Cato, better known as Cato the Elder. He knew Carthage's wealth firsthand and was not shy about his opinions. His speeches in the Senate became famous. No matter what the subject, he ended them the same way: "Ceterum censeo Carthaginem delendam esse" ("Furthermore, I think that Carthage must be destroyed"). He said it so often that it became a joke, but it eventually turned into reality.

Before formally declaring war, Rome imposed increasingly harsh demands on Carthage, pushing its adversary toward submission. A confrontation between Carthage and the Numidians gave Rome its formal pretext, and war was declared. The Romans initially hoped to take the city quickly by force. They were wrong about that. Carthage's walls were formidable, and its defenders were desperate. The siege dragged on for years. It continued until 147 BCE, when Publius Cornelius Scipio Aemilianus arrived in Africa and took command. He moved to cut off supply routes, defeated the Carthaginian field armies operating outside the city, and tightened the stranglehold. Near the end of the siege, Hasdrubal the Boetharch, the commander of the Carthaginian forces, surrendered to Scipio directly.

The assault on the city itself began in 146 BCE. There were six days of brutal street fighting. On the seventh day, the Romans seized the Byrsa, the citadel of Carthage. Hasdrubal had taken refuge with his family in a temple, apparently intending to die there. When the Romans arrived, he instead went to Scipio and asked for mercy. His wife, watching from above, did not spare him her contempt. She condemned him publicly for saving himself, then threw herself and their children into the flames.

The Roman Senate had already decided that Carthage would be destroyed. The decision was not Scipio's to make, though some ancient accounts suggest he felt the weight of what he was witnessing, as a great city was being wiped from existence. Whatever his private feelings, the orders were carried out. Much of the population was sold into slavery. An enormous amount of plunder went to Rome. The territory became the Roman province of Africa (Africa Proconsularis), while other areas were designated *ager publicus* ("public land"), with the local population required to pay tribute. The Numidian kingdom, under Masinissa's sons, expanded into the surrounding lands. Masinissa himself had died during the war at an extreme old age. He was thought to be around ninety, which meant he had outlived almost everyone from the generation that fought Hannibal.

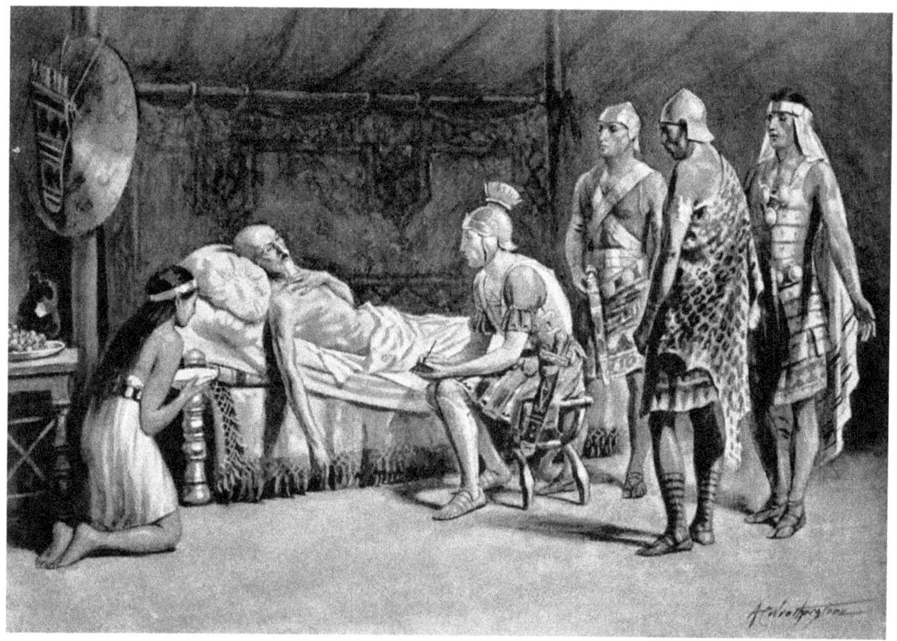

Scipio at the deathbed of Masinissa, by Alfred C. Weatherstone.[10]

What the destruction of Carthage demonstrated was not simply that Rome could win a siege. It showed the extent to which Roman military and political dominance had become total in the Mediterranean world.

Carthage had rebuilt itself from the ruins of the Second Punic War, recovering its wealth and trade networks. It had survived fifty years of Roman pressure and Numidian harassment, and it still was not enough. The city that had once sent Hannibal to the gates of Rome was gone. Scipio Aemilianus received the title Africanus Minor in recognition of the victory, distinguishing him from Scipio Africanus, the general who had won at Zama a lifetime before.

Rome had started as a city on the Tiber surrounded by hostile neighbors. It had spent two centuries fighting for Italy, then another century fighting for the Mediterranean. Now, there was no serious rival left in the west. The next chapter was already beginning.

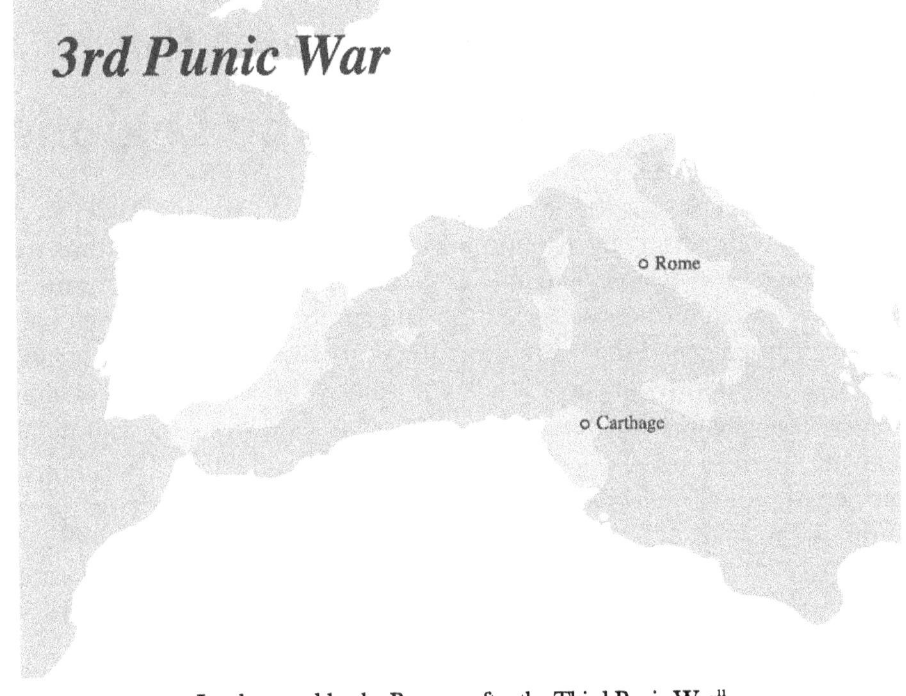

Lands owned by the Romans after the Third Punic War[11]

Chapter 4: Marius and the Professionalization of the Legions

The difficulties facing the Roman army in the 2nd century BCE were bound up with social and economic changes that had been building for generations. As Rome expanded rapidly and warfare grew more expensive, small farmers struggled to maintain their property during long military campaigns. They were away for years at a time, and their land was worked poorly or not at all. An influx of slaves gave wealthy landowners cheap labor for their great estates, known as the latifundia, and the small farming class could not compete with that. The pool of property-holding citizens eligible for conscription may have been shrinking as a result, and the traditional citizen militia was straining to keep pace with the demands being placed on it. Meanwhile, expansion kept requiring more men. The pressure on an already stressed system kept building.

Reform efforts intensified under the Gracchi brothers, particularly with Tiberius Gracchus in 133 BCE. He proposed redistributing public land (ager publicus) that had been illegally occupied by wealthy elites, returning it to landless Roman citizens and, in theory, rebuilding the class of small farmers who formed the backbone of the army. The program was implemented, but many recipients later struggled to maintain their farms under the same economic pressures that had dispossessed people in the first place. The economic instability affecting both the army and the state created fertile ground for corruption and bribery, which further eroded confidence in Roman institutions. The sluggishness of the military response to Rome's problems and the inability to wage wars effectively frustrated Roman society, none more so than the men who actually had to fight them.

One of those men was Gaius Marius, born in 157 BCE. He was a *homo novus*, which means he had no family connections or inherited status. He earned everything himself. He took to military life early and gained distinction as a young soldier under Scipio Aemilianus during the siege of Numantia in 134 BCE. He later served as a military tribune, and after a failed attempt at a magistracy, he worked his way up to quaestor. He was elected tribune of the plebs in 119 BCE. His social standing was modest, but it improved considerably when he married the young Julia, from the noble Julian family, a connection that would take on significance long after Marius himself was gone.

A potential bust of Marius[12]

His chance at something larger came through a crisis in Numidia. After Masinissa's death in 149 BCE, his kingdom was divided among his three sons: Micipsa, Gulussa, and Mastanabal. Gulussa and Mastanabal eventually died, leaving Micipsa to rule alone. Into this situation stepped

Jugurtha, the illegitimate son of Mastanabal. He was ambitious and shrewd, and he had spent time on campaign in Spain watching how the Romans operated, including how Roman officials could be bought.

Micipsa adopted Jugurtha and made him co-heir alongside his own sons, hoping to manage the situation. It didn't work. After Micipsa's death in 118 BCE, Jugurtha employed treachery, assassination, and well-placed bribes to consolidate power. Rome intervened and divided Numidia between Jugurtha and his rival Adherbal following their civil war, giving Jugurtha the western portion. That arrangement lasted only as long as Jugurtha let it.

In Rome, it soon emerged that Jugurtha had bribed numerous officials and even consuls to secure favorable outcomes in the negotiations. The observation he reportedly made about the city, recorded by Sallust, a historian from the Roman Republic, captured what he had concluded from all of it. "[It is] a city for sale and doomed to speedy destruction if it finds a purchaser."[i]

Despite the treaty, Jugurtha quickly attacked the eastern part of Numidia, forcing Rome's hand. The war that followed exposed everything that was wrong with the Roman military establishment at the time. Multiple commanders tried and failed to pin Jugurtha down. He was a gifted guerrilla fighter, and he understood the terrain. He also continued to exploit Roman corruption wherever he found it, which was frequently. The war dragged on far longer than it should have.

Marius served in the campaign as a legate under Consul Quintus Caecilius Metellus. Whatever friction existed between the two men personally—and accounts suggest there was real tension—Marius's abilities were impossible to ignore. He shared meals with his soldiers and worked alongside them, and they respected him for it. In 107 BCE, he was elected consul, a victory seen by many as a rebuke of the corrupt oligarchy that had mismanaged the war. He took over the campaign and, with it, jurisdiction over Metellus's troops.

Marius made real progress where his predecessors had not, but Jugurtha's evasiveness remained a problem. The final solution came through his quaestor, Lucius Cornelius Sulla. Sulla negotiated with Bocchus I of Mauretania, Jugurtha's own father-in-law, who ultimately betrayed Jugurtha and handed him over to the Romans. It was a

---

[i] Sallust, *The Jugurthine War and the Conspiracy of Catiline*, Roman Roads Media, 2015, p.29.

diplomatic coup as much as a military one, and the feat belonged to Sulla—a fact that would sit uneasily between the two men for years afterward.

The capture of Jugurtha[18]

Jugurtha was captured in 105 BCE and paraded in chains through Rome during Marius's triumph. He was then taken to the Tullianum prison and executed in 104 BCE. Ancient sources say strangulation was the method. The Jugurthine War was over after nearly a decade.

What the war left behind mattered as much as its outcome. Jugurtha had not won, but he had succeeded in exposing the rot in the Roman system: the corruption, the favoritism, the willingness of officials to be bought, and the failures of an army structure that had not kept pace with the demands of an empire. Rome had won, but it didn't come out with a great image. The pressure for serious military reform was building, and Marius was the man in the right position to deliver it.

A new threat was already forming on Rome's northern borders. The Cimbri and Teutones, northern tribal groups, had been on the move for years. Their migration stalled when they reached the Balkans, where local resistance pushed them westward and eventually toward Italy's borders. They asked for land within Roman territory in exchange for military submission. The Senate refused, as rulers before them had. That refusal set off a chain of conflicts that Rome handled badly, one after another.

At Noreia in 113 BCE and then, far worse, at Arausio in 105 BCE, the Roman forces were destroyed. At Arausio, tens of thousands of soldiers were lost. The scale of it was shocking even by Roman standards. General after general was sent north and failed. The road into Italy was open, but the tribes had not yet taken it. Why they didn't remains unclear. They turned toward Spain and Gaul instead, which gave Rome the time it badly needed.

The Cimbri are often associated with the Jutland Peninsula, though their exact origins are debated. What is certain is that the migrating tribes had been gathering followers as they moved. Other groups had been absorbed or joined along the way. Ancient sources give figures of up to 200,000 warriors, but modern historians treat those numbers with serious skepticism. The force was large, but it is impossible to say how large.

After his success in Africa, Marius was repeatedly elected consul and given command against the northern tribes. This was an extraordinary concentration of power in one man, but it was justified by the severity of the threat. He used the time before the battle to train and reorganize his forces, preparing them for a kind of warfare that was very different from the desert campaigns against Jugurtha.

The tribes eventually moved into southern Gaul. Marius followed, building fortifications along the route and fighting off their probing attacks without committing to a full engagement. He was waiting. The battle came unexpectedly at first. A detachment of Roman allies, Ligurians, stumbled on the Ambrones bathing in a river, and fighting broke out before any plan had been made. Marius threw his legions in.

The Ambrones were beaten, but the Teutones were still in the hills nearby.

A few days passed. Marius drew his army into battle order on high ground near Aquae Sextiae in what is now southern France. The tribes attacked uphill and were driven back. When they broke and fled, Marcus Claudius Marcellus was waiting in the woods with around three thousand men. He hit them from behind. The slaughter was severe. Later accounts claimed the soil around Aquae Sextiae produced exceptional harvests for years afterward, enriched by the dead. Whether that is true or an embellishment, the battle was a decisive Roman victory.

The Cimbri were still coming, though. Their indecision about when and where to strike gave Marius time to move east and link up with his co-commander, Quintus Lutatius Catulus. The final confrontation came at Vercellae in northern Italy. Boiorix, a leader of the Cimbri, had apparently arranged the time and place with Marius in advance; it would be a formal pitched battle rather than a running fight. Marius positioned his troops so the morning sun was at their backs and in the eyes of the enemy, a small advantage that mattered.

The tribes, reportedly as many as 150,000 strong (though again, ancient numbers should be treated cautiously), advanced and were met with a Roman charge. The battlefield filled with dust. In the chaos, Marius misjudged his own advance and missed the main body of the enemy entirely. It was Catulus, with around twenty thousand men and Sulla leading the cavalry, who absorbed and broke the Cimbrian assault. Exhausted by the summer heat and ground down by tight Roman formations, the tribal warriors collapsed. The battle ended the threat to Rome's northern frontier.

Marius and Catulus shared a triumph, but popular opinion credited Marius as the man who had saved Italy, which irritated Catulus. It likely irritated Sulla too, who had done the hardest fighting at Vercellae.

What Marius had been doing with the army throughout this period was significant. The changes he introduced or that are traditionally associated with him—modern historians debate how systematic or deliberate they were—led to a fundamental shift in how Rome waged war. They built on earlier reform efforts going back to the Gracchi brothers, but they went considerably further.

Before Marius, the army still reflected, at least in theory, the old Servian class structure. Property-owning citizens were organized by wealth, with each providing their own equipment. That model had been showing cracks for decades. Long overseas campaigns were hard for men who had farms to return to, and the pool of eligible citizens may have been shrinking. Marius's changes, beginning after his election as consul in 107 BCE, moved away from that model. Landless citizens, the *capite censi*, those counted by head rather than by property, became eligible to serve. Soldiers were paid a regular wage, the *stipendium*, and military service became a career rather than a civic obligation with a defined end.

Changes in equipment and organization followed. The old distinctions between different grades of infantry, such as the varying arms and armor of different property classes, gave way to something more uniform. All legionaries carried the pilum (javelin) and gladius (sword), wore mail armor and a bronze helmet, and carried a long oval shield. They trained intensively in close-quarters weapons drills. The five old legion standards—a boar, a wolf, a horse, an eagle, and a Minotaur—were replaced with a single silver eagle, the aquila. These men now had a shared identity, similar equipment, and a shared symbol. The esprit de corps that developed was something the old property-based militia had never really had.[i]

The aquila, the symbol of the legion[14]

Cavalry and light infantry (the velites) were increasingly filled by allied and auxiliary troops rather than drawn from the citizen legion itself. The standard auxiliary cavalry unit was the ala, a regiment of around five

---

[i] Esprit de corps is a French phrase meaning cohesion or a common spirit existing in the members of a group, inspiring devotion to a mutual goal.

hundred horsemen, while infantry auxilia were organized into cohorts of a similar size. The primary tactical unit shifted from the maniple to the cohort. A legion's ten cohorts gave the army a flexible building block suited for the varied terrain and enemies Rome was now fighting across the Mediterranean world.

The logistics changed too. The reforms associated with Marius reduced the size of the baggage train, the *impedimenta*, by requiring soldiers to carry more of their own gear. This gave rise to the nickname "Marius's mules," a term for soldiers loaded down with their own equipment. Soldiers had to carry tools for earthworks, including a sickle and a dolabra (pickaxe), cooking utensils, two wooden stakes for field fortifications, a blanket, a coat, and several days' worth of rations. Cattle accompanied the column carrying the heaviest items, mainly the tents and bulk supplies, but the soldiers themselves carried a great deal more than before. The army moved faster because of it.

Among the tactical formations developed in this period was the testudo, the tortoise. Legionaries locked their large shields overhead and around the edges of the formation, creating a shell of overlapping wood and iron that protected against missiles from above. It was slow and cumbersome, but the formation was almost impervious to arrows and stones. When the time came, it could open, and the men inside could charge. It was the kind of disciplined collective maneuver that only a well-trained, cohesive force could execute under fire.

The political consequences of all this were harder to see at the time, although they are obvious in retrospect. When soldiers serve long terms, are paid by their commanders, and depend on those commanders for land grants after being discharged, their loyalty goes to the man rather than the institution. Lucius Appuleius Saturninus, a populist tribune and ally of Marius, pushed legislation through to provide land settlements for Marius's veterans, using violence and intimidation to get it done. In 100 BCE, Saturninus's supporters arranged the murder of a rival candidate. Street violence spread. The Senate invoked the *senatus consultum ultimum* and called on Marius—of all people—to restore order against his own ally. He did it. Saturninus was forced to surrender and took refuge in the Senate building, where a mob got to him anyway.

What that episode revealed was that armed men loyal to a particular general were now a force in Roman politics. As Sallust put it, a soldier "has no regard for his property, having none, and considers anything honorable for which he receives pay."[i] These men were seen as disposable, but they were obedient and grateful to whoever controlled their wages and futures. The veterans were a political bloc. They could be used to gain influence.

The volunteers who filled the new army also gained something beyond pay. Roman citizenship had been extended to many Italian allies, though full citizenship across the peninsula came only after the Social War of 91–88 BCE, and military service was one route into that status. The landless poor could gain wealth, land, and standing in ways that had previously been closed to them. Traditional aristocratic families found their grip on power loosening as men like Marius (*novi homines*, new men without ancient lineage) rose through military achievement.

The first civil war grew out of this transformation. Marius and Lucius Cornelius Sulla had been circling each other since the Jugurthine War, when Sulla's role in capturing Jugurtha had created a tension between them that had never been fully resolved. The flashpoint came over command of the Mithridatic War in 88 BCE. Sulla had been awarded the command as consul. Marius maneuvered to have it transferred to himself. Sulla's soldiers, who were loyal to him, not to the state, feared being replaced by Marius's men. Sulla used that loyalty to do something that had never been done before. He marched his army on Rome itself. Marius fled, and the city fell to Sulla without serious resistance. It was the first time in Roman history that a general had seized power by force of arms.

Sulla set a template. One of the consuls, Cornelius Cinna, later joined with Marius's veterans and retook Rome. The Greek historian Appian's account of what followed is stark. Soldiers "killed remorselessly, and severed the necks of men already dead, parading horrors before the public eye, either to inspire fear and terror, or for a monstrous spectacle."[ii]

The Senate had been losing credibility since the Jugurthine War, when Roman nobles had taken Jugurtha's bribes openly. That damage had never been repaired. What Marius set in motion and what Sulla demonstrated could be done was that the army could override the

---

[i] Sallust, *The Jugurthine War and the Conspiracy of Catiline*, Roman Roads Media, 2015.

[ii] Appian, *The Histories,* Loeb Classical Library, 1913.

Senate entirely. Pompey and Caesar would both use the lesson. The normalization of armed force as a tool of internal politics contributed to the eventual collapse of the Roman Republic, a process that played out over the following decades. Whether it was inevitable is another question. What is clear is that once Sulla marched on Rome, the rules had changed, and everyone knew it.

Chapter 5: Caesar's Gallic Campaigns

Between them, Marius and Sulla broke something that couldn't be fixed. The legions had stopped being Rome's army in any meaningful sense; they were the general's army, loyal to whoever paid them and promised them land when it was over. Once that happened, everything else was a matter of time.

Sulla saw it clearly enough. So did Marius and, later, Caesar. What all three understood, and what the Senate kept failing to grasp until it was too late, was that supreme power in Rome had a prerequisite. One had to

Sculpture of Julius Caesar.[16]

be the best general first. The magistracy, the traditions, the centuries of carefully managed institutional power all meant nothing if someone marched an army through the gates. Marius and Sulla had proved that. Caesar just used the proof.

Caesar's connection to Marius was through marriage. Marius had married Julia, who was Caesar's aunt, which made Caesar Marius's nephew. When Sulla consolidated power in 82 BCE, Caesar's family connections made him suspect. As the nephew of Marius by marriage and the son-in-law of Cinna, he represented the faction Sulla had just defeated. Sulla stripped him of the Flamen Dialis, the priesthood of Jupiter, one of the oldest religious offices in Rome. However, he let him live, which turned out to be the most consequential act of mercy in Roman history.

Caesar survived and eventually escaped Rome, crossing into Asia to serve under the praetor Marcus Minucius Thermus. Away from Sulla's orbit, he started building the thing he actually needed: a reputation. He fought at the siege of Mytilene in 81 BCE on the island of Lesbos, where he distinguished himself enough to be awarded the *corona civica* (the civic crown). He had saved the life of a Roman citizen in battle, and back in Rome, this entitled him to public honors that money couldn't buy. He moved on to Cilicia, serving under Publius Servilius Vatia Isauricus. When Sulla died in 78 BCE, Caesar returned to Rome to begin his political career.

What followed was years of grinding political work. The *cursus honorum*, the fixed ladder of Roman offices, didn't bend for ambition, at least not openly anyway. Caesar spent decades climbing this political ladder. He became a military tribune around 72 BCE, quaestor in 69 BCE, and aedile in 65 BCE. Then, in 63 BCE, he won election as pontifex maximus, making him chief priest of Rome, the senior religious office in the state. He beat out candidates who were far more senior than himself. He became praetor in 62 BCE and then consul in 59 BCE.

The consulship itself was not the real prize, as it only lasted a year. What Caesar wanted was what came after. A proconsular command meant an army, a province, and time. Securing it required backing, which led to his famous alliance with Pompey and Crassus, known as the First Triumvirate. Pompey was the most celebrated general of the age, and Crassus was one of the wealthiest men in Rome. With their support, Caesar obtained command of Cisalpine Gaul and Illyricum, with Transalpine Gaul added shortly after, beginning in 58 BCE. The command was granted for five years initially, but it was extended in 55 BCE.

What Caesar did with this command is documented in his own words. The *Commentarii de Bello Gallico*, his account of the Gallic

Wars, is a detailed military record written in the third person. It is both history and self-promotion. The campaigns ran from 58 BCE to around 50 BCE, primarily covering what is now France, Belgium, and Switzerland. Caesar crossed the Rhine into Germanic territory and landed twice in Britain. The wars built his reputation, filled his war chest with plunder, and gave him the veteran army he would later need for something more ambitious.

Setting the Scene

In 58 BCE, when Caesar took up his command in Gaul, the Roman Republic controlled Hispania, Italia, the Adriatic coast from Istria through the Roman provinces of Macedonia and Achaea in Greece, parts of Asia Minor, parts of Syria and Judea, Cyprus, and the Roman province of Africa (roughly modern Tunisia). A large part of Gaul remained outside Roman control. Caesar was about to change that.

Caesar opens his account by laying out the political geography of the region. The Gauls, members of the broader Celtic grouping of peoples, inhabited roughly modern-day France, Belgium, Switzerland, and parts of northern Italy before the Roman conquest. Caesar divided them into distinct factions and treated each one accordingly. His first focus was the Helvetii, who occupied what is now Switzerland. Around the time Caesar took up his proconsulship, the Helvetii had resolved to migrate westward into Gaul, led by a chieftain named Orgetorix. They burned twelve towns and around four hundred villages behind them to prevent any possibility of turning back. They also gathered neighboring tribes on their move toward western Gaul, attempting to pass through Roman territory near Lake Geneva.

Caesar was not going to allow it. He ordered the construction of a defensive line of trenches and walls stretching from Lake Geneva to the Jura Mountains, roughly nineteen Roman miles in total. While that was being built, he was already working the diplomatic angle, maintaining contact with the Gallic tribes nearest to the Helvetii, namely the Aedui, Sequani, and Santones. These two things together—the capacity to organize large-scale military engineering at speed and the ability to exploit rivalries between Gallic tribes, a strategy often described as "divide and conquer"—were as central to Caesar's success as any battle he fought.

He was a tireless operator. Throughout his years in Gaul, Caesar was constantly in motion, inspecting fortifications, overseeing engagements, negotiating with tribal leaders, and traveling back to Italy to raise fresh legions. Somehow, he also found time to write or dictate the *Commentarii de Bello Gallico*, manage his relationships with Pompey and Crassus back in Rome, and keep a close eye on the political situation in the capital. He was capable of considerable ruthlessness when the situation called for it. The *Commentarii* are full of accounts, told in Caesar's own prose, of massacres and enslavements of Gallic populations.

When it suited him, Caesar was equally capable of framing military action in the language of Roman honor and ancestral obligation. After defeating a portion of the Helvetii, he wrote, "Thus, whether by chance, or by the design of the immortal gods, that part of the Helvetian state which had brought a signal calamity upon the Roman people, was the first to pay the penalty. In this Caesar avenged not only the public but also his own personal wrongs, because the Tigurini had slain Lucius Piso, the lieutenant [of Cassius], the grandfather of Lucius Calpurnius Piso, his [Caesar's] father-in-law, in the same battle as Cassius himself."[i]

The passage is a useful window into how Caesar operated. Caesar was framing a military victory as an act of personal and civic vengeance; the state had been wronged, and so had his family. The two conveniently pointed in the same direction. He was not a hypocrite in any simple sense, but he was also a man who understood that invoking them at the right moment was useful. Caesar's actions played a major role in the collapse of the Roman Republic, and at several points, he faced a choice between his own advancement and the survival of Republican institutions. He chose himself.

But we are getting slightly ahead of the story. The Gallic Wars themselves reveal Caesar's character more clearly than any summary can, and several of their key episodes are worth examining in detail.

Campaigns Against the Tribes

The Helvetii were quite possibly never a genuine threat to the Roman Republic, but Caesar moved against them anyway. They had been heading westward toward the Saône River, and Caesar's forces caught them mid-crossing. The Tigurini, a subgroup of the Helvetii still waiting on the eastern bank, were destroyed. The rest pushed on, and Caesar followed.

[i] Caesar, Julius, *Commentarii De Bello Gallico*, W. J. Gage & Co., 1890, p.7

After dealing with the Tigurini, Caesar moved his troops across the Saône to keep pace with the main Helvetii force. The two armies entered the territory of the Aedui, who were nominally Roman allies, although reluctantly so. Caesar soon uncovered intrigue among the Aedui that was undermining the campaign. Dumnorix, the brother of the pro-Roman noble Diviciacus, was implicated in the affair and was accused of working against Caesar's interests as the campaign progressed. Curiously, Caesar allowed him to live, keeping him under close watch rather than making an example of him, largely out of respect for Diviciacus, who remained loyal.

The Romans followed the Helvetii without a decisive engagement for some time. Roman provisions started to run low, and Caesar began looking toward Bibracte, the Aedui capital, about twenty miles away, as a supply source. The Helvetii got wind of this and turned to pursue the Romans, intending, as Caesar puts it, to "annoy our men in the rear."[i] It is a small detail, but an illuminating one. Modern readers tend to picture ancient warfare as a sequence of grand set-piece battles, with two armies crashing into each other on an open plain. In reality, it was messier and slower. There would be weeks of marching, digging, following the enemy, camping, breaking camp, skirmishing, provoking, and waiting, punctuated occasionally by something that could be called a real battle.

Caesar saw that the Helvetii were growing bolder and looking for an open engagement. He moved his forces to higher ground and arranged them in multiple lines. Then—and he records this himself—he dismounted his horse and ordered his officers to do the same. The message to his men was deliberate. Nobody with a horse was going anywhere. Officers and commanders would fight on foot alongside the rest.

The Helvetii approached. The Romans threw their javelins. This was standard Roman practice, and the pilum was designed with it in mind. Even when it failed to wound or kill, the heavy javelin tended to lodge in an enemy's shield, making it unwieldy and nearly impossible to use. Many Helvetii threw their shields away rather than try to fight encumbered by a javelin shaft. This left them exposed.

The Helvetii began falling back toward a nearby hill where reinforcements were waiting. As the Romans pressed the pursuit uphill,

---

[i] Caesar, Julius, *Commentarii De Bello Gallico*, W. J. Gage & Co., 1890, p. 13

those reinforcements hit them from behind. The Roman force split, with one part facing upward and another part turning to meet the new attack from the rear. The fighting went on into the evening before the Helvetii finally gave way.

After a few days of recovery, Caesar resumed the pursuit. The Helvetii eventually sent envoys to ask for terms. Caesar took hostages and weapons, then ordered them back to their original territory (modern Switzerland). His reasoning, as he explains it, was that the Helvetii served as a buffer against the Germanic peoples to the east, whom Caesar regarded as a threat in their own right. He also recorded figures he claims were found inscribed in Greek on Helvetii territory: 263,000 Helvetii, 36,000 Tulingi, 14,000 Latobrigii, 23,000 Rauraci, and 32,000 Boii. There were 368,000 in total, of whom 92,000 were fighters. Only 110,000 survived by Caesar's count. Caesar likely exaggerated these figures considerably; most modern estimates put the total number of migrants at 150,000 or fewer.

Rome recognized Ariovistus, the king of the Suebi, as a friend and ally of the Roman people. However, in 59 BCE, reports arrived that a hundred Suebi clans were attempting to cross the Rhine into Gaul. Caesar had his justification. The Romans had clashed with Germanic peoples before—the Cimbrian War had happened just a generation earlier—but this was a direct confrontation over control of the Rhine frontier.

In 58 BCE, Caesar moved against Ariovistus. The two forces met somewhere in Upper Alsace near the Rhine. Negotiations failed, and skirmishes between the camps grew more frequent. Ariovistus established a second camp that threatened Roman supply and foraging routes. Facing mounting pressure, Caesar attacked with his six legions and supporting auxiliaries. According to Caesar, the majority of Ariovistus's force, which he puts at 120,000 (a number that is almost certainly inflated), was destroyed. Ariovistus crossed back over the Rhine with a handful of survivors and was not a factor again. Two major threats, the Helvetii and Ariovistus's Germanic coalition, had been dealt with in a single campaigning season. Caesar was well positioned to push further.

His victories in 58 BCE alarmed the tribes of the north. The following year, Caesar marched against the Belgic confederation, which controlled what is now Belgium. Caesar describes them as the fiercest of the Gauls, hardened by constant conflict with the Germanic tribes across the Rhine and, as he notes pointedly, were less exposed to the softening influence of Roman trade and culture. The Belgic coalition put forward various tribal contingents. Caesar claims there were around 288,000 warriors in total, a figure modern historians treat skeptically. Large parts of the confederation submitted without serious resistance as Caesar advanced. The Suessiones, Bellovaci, and Ambiani gave way as he entered their territory. However, the Nervii, along with the Atrebates, Atuatuci, and Viromandui, chose to fight.

At the Battle of the Sabis, Caesar came close to a serious defeat. The Nervii hit the Romans while they were still making camp, catching them before they could form proper battle order. It was one of the most dangerous moments of the entire Gallic campaign. It was resolved only by Caesar's personal intervention on the field and the arrival of reinforcements.

The Atuatuci initially sued for peace and surrendered their weapons—or at least, they appeared to. They had concealed part of their arsenal during the handover. That night, they launched a sortie from the city walls under the cover of darkness, attacking the Roman positions outside. The Romans drove them back. Caesar was not lenient. He had fifty-three thousand of them sold into slavery.

After this, most of the Belgic tribes accepted Roman authority, at least nominally. During the following winter, the Gauls were required to provide grain for Roman troops. In 56 BCE, the Veneti of the northwestern coast rebelled, seizing Roman officials who had been sent to requisition supplies. They had been preparing. Their villages were fortified, positioned on coastal promontories that the tide made nearly inaccessible, and their fleet was built for Atlantic conditions. These were heavy, high-sided vessels with leather sails, suited for rough northern waters in a way that Roman Mediterranean ships were not.

Caesar recognized the problem and appointed Decimus Junius Brutus to build and lead a new fleet. When the two navies met off the Brittany coast, the Romans found a solution to the Venetis' stronger hulls. They used hooked blades on long poles to cut the Veneti rigging, disabling their sails and leaving the heavy vessels unable to maneuver. Without wind, the Veneti ships were helpless, and the Romans picked them off.

On land and without their fleet, the Veneti had no advantage. They surrendered. Caesar executed the tribal elders and enslaved much of the population. He moved against the Morini and Menapii tribes along the coast next, but thick forests and difficult terrain stopped the Roman advance. He let them go.

Attention then shifted to the Rhine. Germanic tribes, the Usipetes and Tencteri, had been driven out of their territory by the Suebi and were attempting to cross into Gaul. Caesar refused their request to settle there. A cavalry engagement followed, in which a Germanic force of around eight hundred horsemen defeated a Roman unit of five thousand. It was an embarrassing defeat. Caesar responded by attacking their camp, killing large numbers of men, women, and children in the process. He claims the dead numbered in the hundreds of thousands. The figure is almost certainly inflated propaganda, but the violence was real and deliberate.

To demonstrate Roman reach, Caesar had his engineers build a bridge across the Rhine in ten days in 55 BCE. The troops crossed, made a show of force in Germanic territory, and returned. The bridge was then destroyed. Caesar did not intend for there to be a conquest; he meant for it to be a statement. Germanic tribes would not find safety simply by crossing the river.

At a meeting of the First Triumvirate known as the Luca Conference, Caesar secured another five years as governor. Pompey and Crassus took the consulship for 55 BCE. With his position secured, Caesar turned to something no Roman commander had attempted: Britain. The island was little known to the Mediterranean world. It was distant, but it had been providing refuge to Gallic leaders who escaped Roman control.

His first attempt, in 55 BCE, was forced back almost immediately by bad weather and the difficulty of landing on an open coast. However, the political effect in Rome was considerable. The Roman public was taken with the idea of armies crossing the ocean. The following year, Caesar returned with a far larger force. He claims he led eight hundred ships of various types. The scale of it was enough that the Britons did not contest the landing. Caesar left Quintus Atrius at the coast with a holding force and pushed inland, extracting tribute from several tribal leaders and installing client kings. Then bad weather struck again, damaging the fleet significantly, and the troops were pulled back to repair it. Caesar withdrew before winter without leaving any permanent garrison.

Britain was not conquered. However, it had been entered, its tribes had formally acknowledged Roman power (even if the tribute they promised was largely theoretical, as no record exists of it actually being paid), and Caesar had stopped British support from reaching the Gauls. More practically, he had added another extraordinary episode to the account he was building of his own campaigns.

A standard bearer of the Tenth Legion leading the Romans to a beach in England[16]

Unrest in Gaul

Crop failures in 54 BCE hit both sides hard. The Gauls were already living under the pressure of Roman occupation, and the food shortage pushed resentment into something more organized. A common cause was taking shape.

The Eburones tribe, under Ambiorix, moved first. He approached Caesar's legate, Quintus Titurius Sabinus, with a warning. Germanic tribes were massing to invade Gaul, and the whole region was on the verge of revolt. If the Romans abandoned their camp and marched out, Ambiorix offered safe passage.

Sabinus believed him. He and his co-commander, Lucius Aurunculeius Cotta, led their men out. However, it was a ploy. They were ambushed in a narrow valley, and both commanders died. Most of the force died too.

The news spread fast. The Nervii, Atuatuci, and other tribes read Sabinus's and Cotta's destruction as a signal and moved against the nearest Roman positions. A force that Caesar puts at around sixty thousand (probably an exaggeration, but it was still large) laid siege to the camp of Quintus Tullius Cicero, brother of the famous orator Marcus Tullius Cicero. The Gauls had learned something about Roman siege methods, partly from watching and partly from Roman prisoners, and they put that knowledge to use. The siege lasted for two weeks.

Caesar, who was still in Gaul, got word and moved quickly, sending two legions to break it. He relieved Quintus Cicero's camp and scattered the attackers. The camp held. Caesar's admiration for Quintus Cicero's conduct during the siege was genuine, as he says so directly in his accounts.

The winter had been brutal, the revolt had been dangerous, and the mood in the Roman command was not good even after the immediate threat was contained. Caesar's response was to go on the offensive. He launched a broad punitive campaign against Ambiorix and the Eburones. He wanted to make an example of them to discourage anything similar from happening again.

It did not fully work. Gallic anxiety and resentment kept building. In 52 BCE, it produced something the Romans had not yet faced in Gaul: a unified, coordinated uprising across multiple tribes, with a single capable leader holding it together.

That leader was Vercingetorix, a young Arvernian nobleman with enough charisma and political skill to assemble a coalition that would normally have been impossible. The Gallic tribes had spent as much of their history fighting each other as fighting anyone else. Getting them to act together required something, and Vercingetorix managed it during the winter of 53–52 BCE. Caesar was in Cisalpine Gaul when he heard about the alliance and moved north immediately.

Vercingetorix fought the war logically, at least at first. He avoided open engagement with Roman legions, concentrated on cutting supply lines and harassing foraging parties, and abandoned towns he judged indefensible rather than lose men trying to hold them. The strategy was sound. The Romans were strong in pitched battles and sieges. If Vercingetorix could keep them hungry and on the move, then he had a chance.

It broke down at Avaricum. The inhabitants refused to burn their own city (one of the most beautiful in Gaul, by Caesar's account), and Vercingetorix reluctantly agreed to defend it. Caesar besieged it in difficult conditions, and the Romans took it. The population was massacred. Vercingetorix's strategic instinct had been right, but he had given in to political pressure and paid for it. Remarkably, the coalition held together anyway. His authority survived the defeat.

The decisive moment came at Alesia. Vercingetorix had gathered a large force. Caesar estimates around eighty thousand men in the town itself, and there was a relief army that he says was much larger, though both figures are probably inflated. Vercingetorix then fortified the hilltop position. Caesar did what Caesar did: he built. The Romans constructed a double ring of circumvallation around the entire hill, miles of fortifications facing both inward toward Alesia and outward toward the relief force that was coming.[i] When the relief army arrived and attacked from outside while the defenders struck from within, Caesar's men held both lines simultaneously. The relief force was broken. The garrison had no way out and nothing left to eat.

Vercingetorix throws down his arms at the feet of Julius Caesar by Lionel Royer[17]

---

[i] Circumvallation is a military tactic that involves building a continuous line of fortified, earthen ramparts and trenches surrounding the besieged city.

Vercingetorix was forced to surrender. He rode out of Alesia in full armor, circled Caesar's position, and dismounted. Caesar held him for six years before bringing him to Rome. He was paraded through the city during Caesar's triumph and executed at the Tullianum prison in 46 BCE.

After Alesia, organized Gallic resistance collapsed. The remaining tribes submitted one by one, and by 50 BCE, Caesar's conquest was effectively complete. Of course, the term "complete" is relative. Caesar had subdued most of Gaul between 58 and 50 BCE, but resistance never fully disappeared. Roman consolidation of the region continued long after he left.

Outside of Caesar's own *Commentarii de Bello Gallico*, which, as you can see, should be read with skepticism, given that Caesar was both the author and the subject, almost no written sources survive for the Gallic Wars. The Gauls kept no written records. Whatever the conflict looked like from their side is gone.

As for Caesar himself, the *Commentarii* reveal a commander who says relatively little about his own physical role in combat. He was present, he was exposed to danger, and he led from the front, but he describes himself as directing and encouraging rather than fighting. Whether that reflects modesty or is simply an accurate self-assessment is hard to say.

In eight years, Caesar had transformed the northwest of the known world. The cultural and political consequences of Roman rule in Gaul lasted for centuries, shaping language, law, and administration across what is now France, Belgium, and beyond.

However, the conquest of Gaul was never really the endpoint. Caesar's command was expiring, his enemies in the Senate were waiting, and the legal protection that his proconsulship had provided was about to disappear. Stripped of his army, he would be a private citizen facing prosecution.

In January 49 BCE, he made a decision that changed everything. He led his Thirteenth Legion across the Rubicon, the river that marked the boundary between his province and Italy proper. Roman law explicitly forbade any general from performing such an act under arms. It was, in effect, a declaration of war against the Senate and the Roman Republic.

Pompey, now Caesar's main rival and the Senate's chosen defender, fled Italy almost immediately. Caesar swept down the peninsula in a matter of weeks, meeting almost no resistance. The civil war that followed lasted four years and took the conflict across the entire Mediterranean world. Caesar won all of it. By 45 BCE, he was back in Rome, where he was appointed dictator perpetuo (dictator in perpetuity), a title with no precedent and no defined end.

The Roman Republic still had a form, but there was not much substance. Caesar held the power, and he showed little interest in pretending otherwise. His military dominance, his concentration of power, and his apparent indifference to Republican tradition drove others to act.

On the Ides of March, 44 BCE, roughly eighty senators and associates, among them Gaius Cassius Longinus and Marcus Junius Brutus, a man Caesar had treated as a close friend and by some accounts something more, surrounded and stabbed him. He was stabbed twenty-three times. His assassins scattered after the attack.

Whether Caesar said anything at the end, and what it might have been, is unknown. The line "Et tu, Brute?" ("You too, Brutus?") comes from Shakespeare's play, which was written sixteen centuries later and has no basis in any contemporary account. It stuck anyway, the way things do when they capture something that feels emotionally true even if it isn't historically real. Whether the assassination was an act of principle or done out of fear or ambition depends on which conspirator you're talking about. What it produced, though, was a power vacuum, and the man who filled it was Octavian.

Chapter 6: Augustus and the Imperial Army

In the wake of Julius Caesar's assassination on March 15th, 44 BCE, chaos gripped the ailing Roman Republic as Caesar's assassins, known as the Liberators, failed to consolidate their hold on Rome and to subdue the pro-Caesar faction, the leadership of which was seized by Caesar's lieutenant Marcus Antonius (commonly known as Mark Antony). Cicero (the famous orator, not the military leader) and the Senate attempted to restrain Antony through political pressure, but the situation was already too far gone for rhetoric, such as Cicero's *Philippics*, to hold. More pressing was the fact that Antony was not Caesar's chosen successor. In his last will and testament, Caesar adopted

Augustus of Prima Porta[18]

his eighteen-year-old grand-nephew, Gaius Octavius, as his son and legal heir.

Gaius Octavius (also known as Octavian, later Augustus) was not an obvious choice for a successor. He came from a wealthy equestrian family, so his lineage was respectable but not part of the old senatorial elite. Octavian had only limited military experience, having served with Caesar in Spain, and was only distantly related to Caesar. However, he did share his grand-uncle's cunning and political acumen, and he was quick to establish himself as Caesar's heir.

Caesar's supporters and, crucially, Caesar's veteran legions came to his side. He also gained the support of the Senate in opposing Antony, who by now was openly fighting Caesar's assassins. Though they clashed at the Battle of Mutina, Octavian and Antony quickly joined forces and unified the pro-Caesar faction against the Liberators. They also recruited Marcus Lepidus, creating the Second Triumvirate in November 43 BCE.

The Triumvirs decisively defeated the legions of Caesar's assassins at the Battle of Philippi in 42 BCE. Brutus and Cassius took their own lives rather than be captured. The three men then divided the Roman Republic between them. Antony took the eastern provinces (Greece, Asia Minor, and Syria), Octavian took the west, including Hispania and Gaul, and Lepidus received Africa. Egypt remained an independent client kingdom under Cleopatra VII, so it was outside Roman provincial administration, though Antony's close ties to Cleopatra gave him significant influence there. Antony and Cleopatra had a political and personal alliance, not a legal marriage, since Antony was married to Octavian's sister, Octavia.

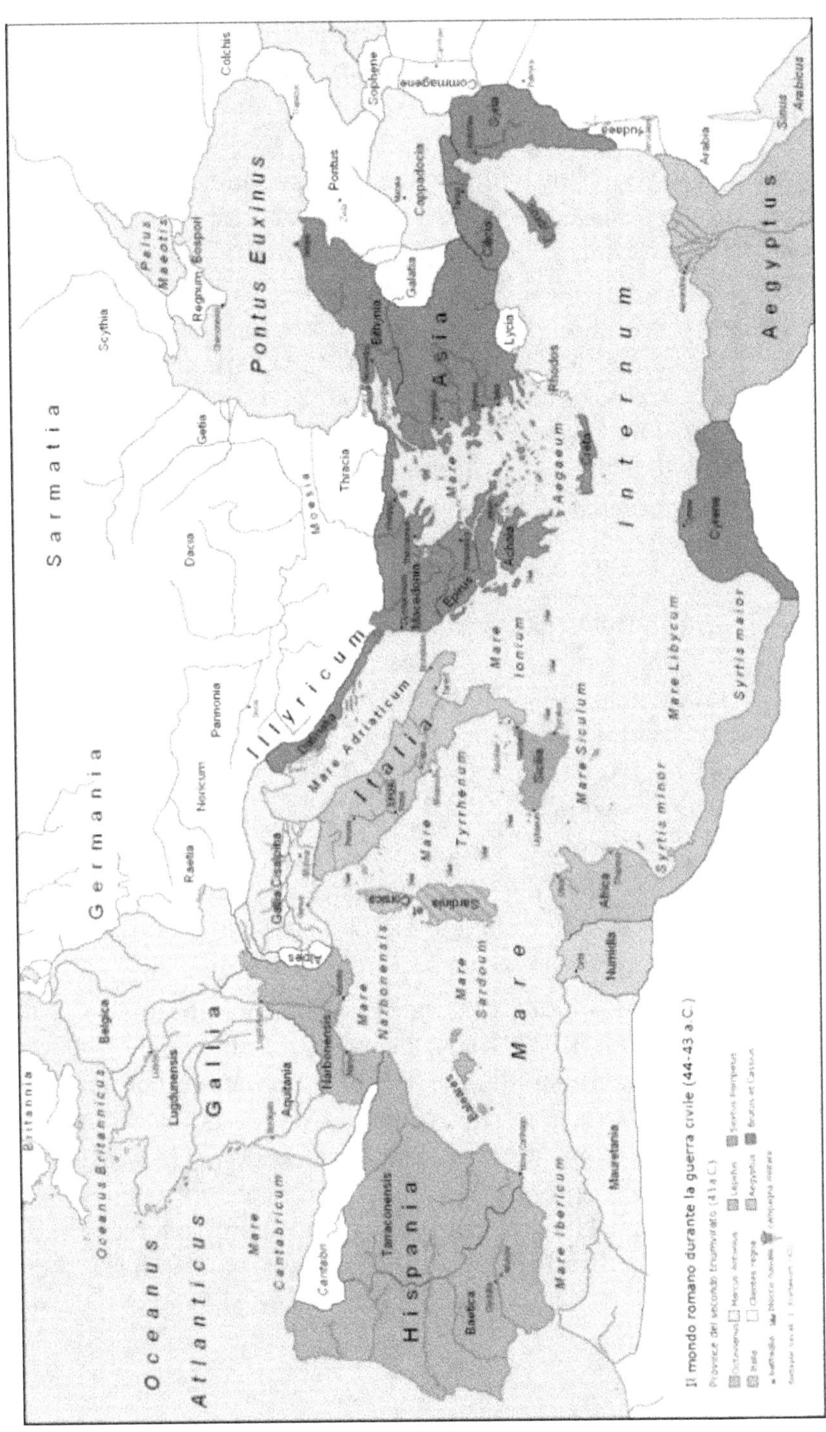

The Roman Empire during the Second Triumvirate[19]

The arrangement was unstable. Apart from the tension between Octavian and Antony, it took Octavian six years to subdue Sextus Pompey, who controlled Sicily and whose fleet threatened Rome's grain supply from Sicily and North Africa. The victory in this campaign was won not by Octavian but by his trusted commander, Marcus Vipsanius Agrippa. Agrippa was a general that any Roman emperor would want on his side. He was loyal, able, and prudent. So many times before, great generals had used their military reputations to reach for sole power. Agrippa could have done the same. He chose not to, though, remaining loyal to Octavian. He was rewarded abundantly. Among other things, he was allowed, and possibly even encouraged, to marry Octavian's daughter Julia. His career is a striking example of the power Roman generals wielded at this time. Agrippa was not simply a military officer. He built the original Pantheon, repaired Rome's aqueducts, and conducted one of the first comprehensive geographic surveys of the empire.

Antony, meanwhile, had barely survived a disastrous campaign in Parthia. With his own position consolidated, Octavian forced Lepidus out of the Triumvirate in 36 BCE. After this, Octavian claimed that "the whole of Italy swore its allegiance to him" and that he was positioned to lead the final confrontation.[i] He claimed allegiance from Gaul, Spain, Africa, Sicily, and Sardinia.

The war against Antony began in 31 BCE. At the naval Battle of Actium, Agrippa's fleet decisively defeated the combined forces of Antony and Cleopatra. Both fled to Egypt, and both took their own lives there the following year as Octavian's forces closed in.

With all political opponents gone, Octavian became the undisputed ruler of Rome, and in 27 BCE, he received the title of Augustus. Modern history remembers him as the first Roman emperor; however, Augustus preserved most of the institutions of the Roman Republic. Though these institutions were severely weakened and placed under his direct control, their preservation was necessary for him to avoid appearing tyrannical. His authority rested on a combination of powers, none of which individually meant autocracy but which together amounted to it. The Senate still met. Augustus just spoke first.

---

[i] Octavianus Augustus, *Res Gestae divi Augusti*, p. 27

Almost two decades of civil war left the legions in a state that Augustus could not ignore. The problem wasn't just the military; it was also political. Armies in the late Roman Republic had been loyal to their commanders, not the state. Augustus intended to redirect that loyalty toward the princeps and the imperial institution itself.[i]

Marcus Claudius Marcellus, Augustus's nephew through his sister Octavia and later his son-in-law after marrying Augustus's daughter Julia, was gaining some following and could plausibly be positioned as a successor, which made the Senate nervous. Fears of a monarchical dynasty fed a conspiracy against Octavian in 23 BCE. That year proved to be a turning point. After surviving the conspiracy, Augustus fell seriously ill. Suetonius claims he came close to giving up entirely, but Augustus recovered and pushed through a significant restructuring of his own power. He gave up the consulship and instead consolidated authority through a combination of powers: tribunicia potestas, which gave him the rights of a tribune of the plebs, and imperium proconsulare maius, authority over the provincial armies, which meant he outranked any other commander. Combined with his status as princeps, these made him the dominant force in the state.

He was, formally, "first among equals." In practice, after 23 BCE, he had something very close to absolute power. The title imperator, which he had already used as part of his name, though it did not yet carry the meaning of "emperor" in any modern sense, became permanently attached to the office. Every ruler after him bore it. By controlling the army and representing the citizens, something later emperors would fail at spectacularly, Augustus paved the way for autocracy. Even though Rome was still formally a republic during his reign, Augustus had managed to achieve what Caesar and every ambitious general before him had not. He became, in every meaningful sense, the first Roman emperor.

Military reforms followed. First, he reduced the military from over fifty legions raised during the civil wars down to twenty-eight. The basic composition of a legion stayed largely the same. It comprised around five thousand heavy infantry who were armored and fought with the gladius and pilum. The legion was still organized into cohorts and centuries. What changed was the nature of the soldier himself. Augustus's legions were to be volunteer professionals, not mobilized

------

[i] Princeps means "the first" or "most eminent."

citizens. These men would be better trained, serve longer terms, and receive better logistical support. Dedicated and expanded logistical support meant a Roman legion could sustain itself in the field for seasons while deep in enemy territory, though seizing local supplies remained standard practice on a campaign regardless. Engineering capability was built in as well. Legionaries were expected to fight and also build fortifications, winter quarters, bridges, roads, and earthworks.

Twenty-eight legions could not cover everything. Other roles, including cavalry, scouts, archers, slingers, and border garrisons, needed to be filled, and this was where the auxilia came in. These were professional units recruited from non-citizens across the empire. Certain regions became associated with particular skills. For instance, the Balearic Islands were famous for their slingers, the best archers came from Crete and Syria, and Numidia was known for its light cavalry. Auxiliary units were roughly cohort-sized, ranging from five hundred to a thousand men depending on their role, which gave them both strategic and tactical flexibility. They could be attached to legions for major campaigns or spread across borders in peacetime. This smaller size also meant the foreign-composed auxilia would rarely, if ever, approach the numerical strength of the more politically reliable citizen legions nearby, even though at their peak, auxiliaries made up a substantial portion of the total Roman army. They were generally stationed outside their home regions, partly to prevent rebellion and partly to push assimilation into Roman military culture.

The need to protect the emperor personally and to maintain loyalty close to home was reflected in the founding of the Praetorian Guard. These men were recruited primarily from Italy, and they formed a distinct elite unit. Their role was to protect the emperor both on campaign and in Rome itself, where they were frequently the only military force present. Augustus had no major troubles with his Praetorian Guard. His successor, Tiberius, was considerably less fortunate. The Praetorians' close proximity to the emperor made them a political force in their own right, so they were effectively in a position to influence who lived and who didn't.

Augustus's reforms did not happen in a vacuum; they took place against the backdrop of almost continuous frontier warfare. Practically every year of his reign involved at least one significant military campaign, whether for conquest or suppressing a revolt. One of the early campaigns was the Cantabrian Wars (29–19 BCE). Augustus wanted to bring the last unconquered part of northern Hispania under Roman control. This wasn't a single war but a series of conflicts stretching across a decade. The difficulty wasn't the Romans' inability to fight; it was terrain and guerrilla tactics. The tribes of the region were skilled with light weapons, and the mountains made supply chains a constant problem. Augustus eventually committed eight legions, some thirty thousand soldiers, plus twenty thousand auxiliaries and naval support, to finish the job. Roman sources claim the Asturians preferred to die by their own hand rather than be taken prisoner. Death in arms was a form of victory in their opinion, and the Romans had little use for slaves who thought this way. Main resistance ended in 19 BCE, with smaller conflicts continuing until around 13 BCE.

Campaigns in northeastern Gaul (modern Belgium and the Netherlands) pushed the border to the Rhine, and fighting in the Balkans brought the frontier to the Danube. These two rivers would mark the limits of Roman power in Europe for centuries. Galatia, in what is now Turkey, was annexed in 25 BCE. Rebellions in Africa, Egypt, and Syria were pacified and settled.

As the empire expanded, new problems emerged. Tensions along the German frontier had been building, and by 12 BCE, the Germanic tribes near the mouth of the Rhine had been forced to acknowledge Roman authority. Augustus wanted more. He wanted a permanent Roman presence east of the Rhine. He gave the task to his stepson, Nero Claudius Drusus, who pushed Roman forces as far east as the Elbe by 9 BCE before dying that year after a riding accident. His brother, Tiberius, the future Roman emperor, took over and ran a successful campaign, though the province of Germania never really stabilized into anything resembling proper Roman provincial administration.

The Roman Empire under Augustus before the Pannonian revolt[20]

The plan after that was to push south into the territory of the Suebian kingdom under Maroboduus. Augustus began assembling a large army for a two-pronged attack. That plan collapsed when Pannonia erupted in revolt. The Illyrian tribes there were deeply unhappy with Roman taxation and military recruitment. Ancient sources put the rebel forces at around 200,000 infantry and 9,000 cavalry; although these figures are probably generous, the tribes still represented a serious threat.

Augustus reportedly told the Senate that if extreme measures were not taken immediately, the rebel army could reach Rome within days. Veterans were recalled to service. Slaves were freed and enlisted. Tiberius was put in command. Rather than seeking pitched battles, he controlled key positions and launched targeted strikes, grinding the revolt down over the years rather than breaking it in a single campaign. It worked, but it was slow and expensive.

The toll showed. The rebellion disrupted supply chains and triggered an economic crisis across the affected regions. Augustus's policies toward the newly conquered tribes were harsh, which deepened resentment rather than settling it. Even the equites, the wealthy citizen class that had generally supported Augustus, were unhappy. Dissatisfaction spread to the Senate and down to the plebs. The reputation Augustus had built over decades of stable, successful rule began to take a hit.

While Tiberius was still managing the Pannonian revolt, news came from Germany. Publius Quinctilius Varus, the governor charged with administering Roman territory east of the Rhine, had been ambushed and destroyed. Arminius, a chieftain of the Germanic Cherusci tribe who had been raised in Rome, trained in the Roman army, and held Roman citizenship, had spent years convincing Varus of his loyalty. One day, he led three Roman legions into the Teutoburg Forest and into a trap that had been carefully prepared. The legions were massacred. Varus killed himself. It was one of the worst military disasters in Roman history and the greatest humiliation of Augustus's reign. His reported response has become famous: "Quintili Vare, legiones redde!" ("Quintilius Varus, give me back my legions!").

Germanic warriors storming the field[21]

The disaster is sometimes framed as a consequence of Roman overreliance on foreign auxiliaries, but that explanation misses most of what actually happened. Poor intelligence, terrain that neutralized Roman tactical advantages, overconfidence, and Arminius's carefully maintained deception were the real causes. There had been similar episodes during Caesar's campaigns in Gaul, but the scale of the Teutoburg failure was unprecedented. The Roman army had not suffered a defeat this serious since Hannibal's victories in the Second Punic War.

Roman operations in Germany did not stop entirely after Teutoburg. Tiberius continued to campaign in the region, and after Augustus's death in 14 CE, Germanicus, son of the original Drusus, pushed further still under Tiberius's reign, with campaigns running into 16 CE. Augustus, however, had made his position clear before he died: the Rhine and Danube were where Roman expansion should stop. In the last years of his reign, he settled roughly half of all Roman legions along those two frontiers. That defensive posture in the West became the template for the emperors who came after him.

Earlier in his career, Augustus had been involved in Roman affairs in the East, namely Armenia, Syria, and Egypt, although he had dealings with Parthia and various client rulers. He directed policy and diplomacy there instead of personally campaigning. His attitude toward Eastern religions and cults was negative. Greek culture was treated differently, sitting just below Roman culture in the official hierarchy and receiving considerably more respect. Augustus revived old Roman religious customs and festivals, such as the Fratres Arvales and the Sodales Titii, and reformed the religious magistracies.

The reign of Augustus was as much a turning point in Roman history as it was a pivot of ancient history more broadly. His moderation and willingness to reward those close to him meant that there were no traitors in his inner circle. That was filled only with men he could trust to do their jobs. He was a man of broad enough view to understand that different situations called for different methods. He never abandoned Roman expansionism, but he knew when to stop, which was a skill the Roman Republic's generals had never quite developed. The institutional framework he built, the frontier decisions he made, and the foreign policy patterns he established all set the shape of the empire that followed him. The territory Rome controlled would grow larger in the centuries after him, but the pillars of how Rome would manage and defend that territory were put in place during his reign.

Chapter 7: Pax Romana: The Roman Army at Its Zenith

The period historians label the Pax Romana (the Roman Peace) is something of a misnomer. Rome frequently waged wars throughout this period in every corner of the empire. What the term actually refers to is internal peace and stability, especially when set against the intense civil unrest and military chaos that preceded and followed it. That internal order was maintained by the large professional armies of legions and auxilia manning Rome's borders and fighting its wars of conquest.

Augustus's campaigns had pushed the empire's frontiers to the Rhine and Danube. Further expansion into Germania was stopped decisively at the Battle of the Teutoburg Forest in 9 CE, where Arminius, a Germanic tribesman with Roman military training, destroyed three legions and their commander. Military activity in the region continued regardless, running until 16 CE, driven partly by the desire to avenge Teutoburg.

Augustus had reorganized the auxilia into a permanent corps of non-citizen soldiers around 27 BCE, building on auxiliary forces that had existed in the Roman Republic but formalizing and standardizing them for the first time. They were recruited mainly from the *peregrini*, free provincial subjects without Roman citizenship, as well as from peoples beyond the empire's borders whom Romans collectively termed "barbarians," a word derived from the Greek for "foreigner." The term basically meant someone outside of the Roman civilization, though it often carried the sense of being uncivilized. These non-citizen soldiers were regularly stationed in provinces other than where they had been raised, partly to encourage Romanization and partly to reduce the risk of local loyalties overriding military loyalties. The names of auxiliary units persisted long after the original recruits were gone, and by the later empire, auxiliary soldiers were often comparable to legionaries in training and capability, though their equipment and roles sometimes differed.

The most prominent Roman commander of this period was Germanicus Julius Caesar. He was not a descendant of Julius Caesar, but he carried the name as part of the imperial family naming system that Augustus's adoption had set in motion. He was the nephew and adopted son of Emperor Tiberius. Germanicus defeated Germanic forces in several engagements, including the Battles of Idistaviso and the Angrivarian Wall, and recovered two of the three legionary aquilae (the eagle standards) lost in the forests of Teutoburg. These were real military achievements, though they did not result in permanent Roman control of Germania east of the Rhine. It was because of these campaigns that he received the agnomen Germanicus. He died in Syria in 19 CE.

Germania beyond the Rhine remained unconquered, aside from the fertile plains of the Lower Rhine and the strip of territory between the Rhine and Danube. The reasons were straightforward enough. Central Europe was far more heavily forested than it is today, the population was hostile, the region offered little material wealth compared to other areas, and there were no natural defensible borders to anchor a frontier. Holding the Limes Germanicus, the Germanic frontier, would remain one of the Roman army's longest and most difficult commitments for the rest of the empire's existence.

The next major campaign was the conquest of Britain, beginning in 43 CE under Emperor Claudius. It lasted over forty years in its main phase, although Roman campaigns in Britain persisted for decades after the initial conquest. Although Hadrian's Wall was built in the early 2nd century CE to stabilize the northern frontier, fighting in northern Britain went on well beyond it.

Rome's eastern border with Parthia was also under a lot of pressure, with wars running from 59 to 64 CE and continuing throughout the 1st century. Revolts added to the strain. The Great Jewish Revolt brought widespread destruction to the province of Judaea from 66 to 74 CE. Near the Rhine Delta, the Batavi tribe rose in 70 CE and destroyed two full legions before a large Roman force finally suppressed them. In Britain, Iceni Queen Boudica staged a revolt that came closer to succeeding than Rome would have liked to admit. These uprisings had different causes and contexts. Many stemmed from local political and economic grievances that had been building for years, though some were also shaped by the instability running through the empire during this period, particularly the civil wars of 69 CE.

That year, known in Roman history as the Year of the Four Emperors, was the first major imperial civil war involving multiple rival claimants to the throne since the time of Augustus. It was brief, but it showed that the principate was not as settled as it had appeared and that the army remained the ultimate arbiter of power. Vespasian, who prevailed, had the broadest military backing of any of the claimants, built in large part on his own record and his son Titus's conduct during the Jewish Revolt. He founded the Flavian dynasty, which replaced the Julio-Claudians. He ended five generations of stepsons, nephews, and adopted heirs who had ruled from Augustus until Nero.

The empire reached its greatest geographical extent under Trajan (r. 98-117), whose Dacian campaigns and later push into Mesopotamia extended Roman rule as far as the Persian Gulf. Augustus had believed that victory was the precondition for peace. His own formulation of it, recorded in the *Res Gestae*, described a peace won through conquest: "Per totum imperium populi Romani terra marique ... parta victoriis pax" ("Throughout the whole Roman Empire, on land and sea, a peace won by victories"). The coins of the period bore the inscription Pax Augusti, "Augustus's peace." It was not a peace achieved by standing still.

A Roman coin from 243-244 stating "Pax Augusti" on the reverse[28]

The Pax Romana represents the peak of Roman military capability, though that phrase needs unpacking. Military capability is not simply a matter of how well individual soldiers fight or what armor they wear. The lorica segmentata, the segmented metal armor most associated with the Roman soldier of this period, was not objectively superior to everything it faced. For instance, Roman soldiers in the Dacian Wars suffered serious wounds from the falx, a two-handed Dacian bladed weapon capable of getting under or around conventional armor. Even at the height of Roman dominance, defeat was not unknown.

A recreation of the lorica segmentata[34]

What made the imperial Roman army of the Pax Romana exceptional was its ability to operate across the full extent of the empire, sometimes on multiple frontiers at the same time, in practically any climate or season, and to sustain itself in hostile territory for extended periods, often years. That kind of capability depended on a set of disciplines that went well beyond individual fighting skills. Logistics—producing or foraging and then moving adequate supplies—was foundational. Intelligence gathering, military engineering, the ability to construct roads, bridges, fortifications, and siege equipment in the field all contributed to what made a Roman army effective rather than just large.

On the broader scale, the empire had to maintain a manpower pool large enough to fill professional armies and a farming base capable of feeding them in peacetime. It needed an economy stable enough to pay regular salaries and equip hundreds of thousands of soldiers continuously. Estimates suggest that somewhere between 50 and 70 percent of the imperial budget went to the military. It was the dominant expense of the Roman state for the remainder of its existence, and everything else was built around it.

Behind just one legion of some five thousand fighting men stood a vast support structure. There were non-combat personnel, mules, horses, wagons, attendant slaves, camp followers, sutlers (merchants who followed armies to sell goods), cooks, and craftsmen. At full strength, around five hundred soldiers in a legion, roughly 10 percent, were immunes, or dedicated specialists excused from some routine duties and paid better for it. These men were still trained legionaries, so they were capable of fighting when needed. They included engineers, artillerymen, drill instructors, carpenters, medics, and surveyors.

This professional core meant that a Roman army in the field during the principate was, in both peace and war, effectively a traveling construction crew. On campaign, the army built roads as it advanced, allowing for reinforcements, resupply, and retreat. Roman road-building was good enough that some roads survive today. Many modern European routes follow the general alignments of roads the Romans laid down two thousand years ago.

Military construction went well beyond roads. Over three hundred fortresses were erected along the Rhine and Danube alone, plus countless castra (forts and legionary quarters), many of which grew into cities over the centuries. London, Cologne, and Belgrade started as Roman military installations. The Romans also perfected the large-scale construction of durable load-bearing bridges, particularly stone arch bridges, building them in permanent stone, in wood, and as pontoon crossings. Many stone bridges survive today; some are still even used. Others are known only through records, such as Caesar's two wooden bridges across the Rhine and Trajan's bridge across the Danube, the longest bridge in antiquity at over a kilometer in length.

During the nearly two centuries of the Pax Romana, the Roman army, as it had done before and would continue to do afterward, adapted constantly, taking on new roles, developing new tactics, and finding ways to counter what enemies threw at it. This period saw the full development of the Roman legionary as heavy armored infantry. They used the gladius, scutum, and pila. They fought in tight formations where soldiers supported one another and exhausted front-line troops could be rotated to the rear and replaced with fresher men. Against the most common infantry opponent of the period—a non-professional fighter with a spear and shield—a disciplined Roman formation in open ground had a decisive advantage. The original manipular system had been developed, after all, to counter the Greek phalanx.

The problem was that the battles the Romans wanted to fight were relatively uncommon. Many of Rome's enemies understood Roman tactics well enough to avoid pitched battle when possible, which meant the Romans often had to fight on worse terms, with exposed flanks or on difficult terrain, or take what they wanted through siege. Roman soldiers became capable of constructing elaborate siegeworks and manufacturing a range of siege weapons, like the *scorpio* and ballista for medium-range fire and, later, the onager for heavier bombardment. They also used scaling ladders, siege towers, and battering rams.

The Romans learned from disasters. The Battle of Carrhae in 53 BCE, where Crassus's legions were destroyed by Parthian cavalry, highlighted the Romans' vulnerability to mobile horse-mounted armies. The fast-moving horse archers and heavily armored cataphracts were the enemies that Rome kept encountering on the eastern frontier. Legionaries already had anti-cavalry responses, such as the square formation and using pila as spears to extend their reach against riders, but Carrhae sharpened the emphasis on discipline when facing mounted attacks. It also pushed the Roman cavalry, which was largely drawn from foreign auxilia, toward greater tactical standardization. They would begin to regularly harass enemy cavalry, protect friendly infantry, and keep the flanks clear. In Britain, chariot-mounted archers and javelin throwers posed a different kind of problem, and Roman tactics adjusted there too.

The Teutoburg disaster led to improvements in scouting. Roman armies in the field operated with several layers of intelligence-gathering. Exploratores worked ahead of the column, reconnoitering the ground. Speculatores ranged farther still, operating well ahead of the army and sometimes behind enemy lines; they were intelligence agents as much as scouts. The procursatores covered the army's immediate surroundings. Together, they gave Roman commanders a picture of enemy positions, movements, and strength that most opponents simply couldn't match. That intelligence advantage translated directly into initiative.

None of it would have worked without discipline. Josephus, who watched the Roman army train, wrote that their drills were no different from the real thing. He called them bloodless battles, while their actual battles were bloody drills.[i] The first thing a recruit learned was the military pace and his place in formation. Training began with wooden weapons and then progressed to mock battles. Cavalry developed a complex sequence of drills known as the hippika gymnasia. Roman training emphasized both individual skill and coordinated unit performance to an unusual degree. Most enemies had experienced warriors, but the Romans had something those warriors generally did not: the ability to function as a unit under pressure.

In actual combat, casualties during the main phase of close engagement were relatively light on both sides since each side's soldiers were protecting and being protected by those next to them. Wounded men could be pulled back. The real danger was a flank or rear attack, which threatened not just physical vulnerability but psychological cohesion. Enough disruption would lead to panic, panic would lead to a rout, and a routed army would break apart and be slaughtered piecemeal. Roman discipline reduced the likelihood of routs, though they did occasionally occur. Professional soldiers accustomed to combat conditions were simply less likely to break, and if they were losing, they often kept fighting rather than running. Even during construction work, this discipline held. Legionaries building a fortified camp were expected to be able to drop their tools and repel an attack.

The Roman army fought, almost as a rule, to keep the initiative. They were to stay on the offensive and force the enemy to respond. When the empire's later history forced Rome into an increasing number of defensive wars, the legionary system of the Pax Romana found itself poorly adapted to the new situation. Holding a static frontier was not what it had been built for.

The end of the Roman Peace came from several directions at once. The Antonine Plague, which lasted from 165 to 180 CE, tore through

---

[i] Josephus, Flavius, *Wars of the Jews.*

the empire's population and disrupted the manpower available to the legions. The economic consequences were severe. Emperor Marcus Aurelius responded by devaluing the currency, reducing the silver content of the denarius, which generated short-term revenue at the cost of longer-term stability. Plus, the currency had already been debased multiple times before. He did it to pay the army. Everything else in the economy suffered for it, though, and the inflation that followed made the underlying instability worse. The Marcomannic Wars on the Upper Danube dominated Marcus Aurelius's reign, and before that, his co-emperor, Lucius Verus, had fought an expensive war against Parthia. Both were won, but both drained resources that Rome could not easily replace.

Marcus Aurelius was succeeded by his son Commodus, who made things worse rather than better. He was assassinated in 193, the Year of the Five Emperors. Roman legionaries once again clashed against each other in civil war, and a series of assassinations and armed conflicts shook the empire's political structure. The crisis was eventually contained under Septimius Severus, the last man standing from that year's succession struggle. However, the long-term consequences for the army were significant.

The distinction between citizen legionaries and non-citizen auxilia was gradually eroded after the Constitutio Antoniniana, also known as the Edict of Caracalla, of 212. Septimius's successor, Caracalla, extended full Roman citizenship to every free man in the empire. The reasons behind it are still debated. He could have been expanding the tax base since full citizens paid more, broadening the manpower pool for the legions, or building personal loyalty to the man who had granted citizenship. It was probably some combination of all three.

In 216, Caracalla launched a campaign against Parthia. He was assassinated within the year. His successor, Macrinus, lasted less than a year. He was overthrown without ever visiting Rome to be confirmed by the Senate, and his attempts to stabilize the economy at the army's expense predictably ended in military revolt. Elagabalus, who followed, did little to reverse the decline. His successor, Severus Alexander (r. 222–235), made real progress in stabilizing the empire's fortunes, but when he was assassinated in 235, Rome entered the Crisis of the Third Century, a period of near-continuous civil war and external pressure that transformed the empire almost beyond recognition.

The concept of the Pax Romana outlasted Rome itself. Later empires, Byzantine and in the Christian West, looked back on the period as a model worth imitating, even if they never quite managed to reproduce it.

Chapter 8: Decline and Fall: Military Challenges in Late Antiquity

The peace did not collapse overnight, but the death of Marcus Aurelius in 180 CE is generally taken as the symbolic end of the Pax Romana. What followed was a period of political, military, and economic crisis for the empire and for the army that held it together.

Aurelius was succeeded by his son Commodus, who was an ineffective and self-indulgent ruler. The contrast with the so-called Five Good Emperors was stark.[i] Those men had come to power through adoption and selection on merit, or something close to it. Later emperors came through coups, bribery, and assassination.

Lucius Septimius Severus was a product of that new reality. He gained power through the army, and the army remained the foundation of everything he did. Cassius Dio attributes these words to him: "Get along, pay the soldiers substantially, and don't worry about the rest."[ii] He fought a long civil war to secure his position and pushed through significant reforms once he had it. For instance, he dismissed the existing Praetorian Guard and replaced it with soldiers personally loyal to him. He also campaigned against the Parthians. He died in 211 during a campaign against the Caledonians in Britain.

---

[i] The Five Good Emperors were Nerva, Trajan, Hadrian, Antoninus Pius, and Marcus Aurelius.

[ii] Mashkin, Nikolai, *A History of Ancient Rome,* Gospolitizdat, 1956, p. 363

Severus was succeeded by his two sons, Marcus Aurelius Antoninus, known to history as Caracalla, and Publius Septimius Geta. Both were recognized as co-rulers, but Caracalla quickly emerged as the dominant one. He had Geta murdered not long after, becoming the sole ruler. He spent money the empire didn't have trying to buy off enemies and secure loyalty, but it wasn't enough. In 217, he was assassinated as part of a conspiracy organized by the Praetorian Prefect Macrinus.

Political instability after that became something close to the norm. The mid-3rd century crisis, running roughly from 235 to 284, saw more than twenty emperors and numerous usurpers rule in the space of fifty years. Most of them died violently. They were frequently killed by the same soldiers who had elevated them. Civil war was almost continuous. Financial pressure made everything else worse.

The military consequences were severe. Germanic raiders pushed deep into the western provinces. The East was overrun in large parts by the Sassanid Persians, who had replaced the Parthians as Rome's main eastern rival and were considerably more aggressive. In 251, Emperor Decius was killed when his army was defeated by the Goths; it was the first time a reigning Roman emperor had died in battle against a foreign enemy. In 260, Valerian was captured by the Persians. Two breakaway states emerged during this period: a short-lived Gallic Empire in the west and the Palmyrene Empire in the east, centered on the Kingdom of Palmyra, both of which temporarily held large chunks of what had been Roman territory. Meanwhile, civil wars kept draining the army's capacity to deal with any of it.

Valerian's son Gallienus, already a joint ruler since 253, succeeded him. His reign was defined by one crisis after another, and he was killed in 268 during one of the many uprisings against him. The soldiers chose Claudius II as his replacement. He moved quickly. His first major engagement was against the Alamanni, who had pushed into Italy. He defeated them at the Battle of Lake Benacus in 268, earning the title Germanicus Maximus for it. Then he turned east to deal with the Goths in the Balkans.

He found their army at Naissus, in what is now Serbia, in 269. The battle was hard and bloody. The Romans broke the Gothic force partly through a feigned retreat, drawing them out of position before hitting them from prepared positions. The future emperor Aurelian apparently played an important role in the final stages of the fighting, though the victory belonged to Claudius as much as anyone. Tens of thousands of

Goths were killed or captured. It was the kind of decisive result the empire badly needed. However, the rest of the empire was still burning, and Claudius did not live long enough to deal with it; he died shortly after Naissus, probably of plague. His brother Quintillus took the throne and lasted only weeks before the legions around Sirmium declared for someone else entirely.

That someone was Aurelian, later called the Restitutor Orbis ("Restorer of the World"). He was a barracks emperor, which means the legions proclaimed him emperor. The loyalty of his soldiers brought him to power rather than his birth or senatorial backing. His father had worked as a tenant farmer for a senator in the Roman province of Pannonia in the Balkans, which was not exactly the traditional background for an emperor. Earlier emperors had typically come from the senatorial aristocracy, while the 3rd century increasingly produced emperors who had risen entirely through their military careers. Aurelian was the fullest expression of that pattern.

That pattern itself is worth pausing on because it represents one of the most significant structural shifts of the entire period. The great commanders of earlier centuries—Marius, Sulla, Pompey, Antony, Caesar, Augustus, and Germanicus—had all been tied to the highest aristocratic networks from birth. Military talent and aristocratic connections went together. Vespasian had been an early crack in that pattern. He was not from the old elite and had to fight his way to the throne through the chaos of 69 CE. The military became the primary route to imperial power. Anyone with enough soldiers and enough ability to hold their loyalty could try for it, and many did.

The consequences of this ran deep. As rivals for the throne spent more time with provincial armies, those armies started behaving more like personal retinues. The composition of senior officer ranks shifted. Senatorial representation declined steadily through the 3rd century, replaced by equestrian career soldiers who had spent their lives in the army and held no civil offices. These were the men most likely to plot against sitting emperors and put forward candidates from their own circles. Emperors spent so much time on campaigns that they became increasingly distant from Rome and Roman political life. The court moved with the army. To become emperor, one needed popularity with the troops and the ability to lead them in battle. That was more or less it. And because that was the qualification, no emperor could safely hand command of a major army to a potential rival, unlike the old consular system, where military command was transferred on a fixed schedule, whether anyone liked it or not. The result was paranoia, fragmentation, and a cycle of rebellion that fed on itself.

Aurelian saw all of this clearly and somehow managed to cut through it. He reunited the empire, reconquering the Palmyrene territories in the east and suppressing the Gallic breakaway state in the west, and held it together through a combination of military force and political reform. He elevated the cult of Sol Invictus, the Unconquered Sun, building a major temple in Rome and promoting it. The cult had existed before his reign, but Aurelian gave it unprecedented prominence within the imperial religious system. The symbolism was clear. A single sun ruling the heavens could serve as a powerful metaphor for a restored and unified empire.

He also turned to the food supply. Rome had a long tradition of subsidized grain distribution for the poorest citizens, dating back to the Roman Republic, but Aurelian expanded it significantly, switching from raw grain to baked bread and, in some cases, adding other commodities such as oil, pork, and salt. Keeping the urban poor fed was both a genuine welfare measure and a practical political calculation, and Aurelian was clear-eyed enough to pursue both at once. It earned him real popularity in the city.

He knew there would be more usurpers. There always were. He spent his reign moving between suppressing rebellions and implementing reforms, never fully separating the two problems because they could not really be separated. The crisis that had consumed the 3rd century was not solved by any single campaign or any single reform. What Aurelian did was stabilize enough of it to give the empire a foundation to build on, which is why the title Restitutor Orbis stuck.

After several decades of crisis, a measure of stability returned under Diocletian. He held off foreign invaders, and the reforms he pushed through, some of which were already in motion under his predecessors, addressed both the political and military foundations of the empire. His most significant innovation was the Tetrarchy, a system of divided imperial power with two senior emperors, each titled Augustus, ruling the Eastern and Western halves respectively. They would be supported by a junior colleague called Caesar. The idea was practical on two levels. There would be enough commanders to handle simultaneous crises across a vast empire and a built-in succession system that gave ambitious men with armies a legitimate path forward rather than a reason to rebel.

Diocletian managed to reduce, at least for a time, the constant threat of assassination and forced abdication that had defined the previous half-century. Elite court units, such as the *protectores domestici*, developed during this period. The Praetorian Guard continued to exist until it was abolished by Constantine in 312.

Diocletian and Maximian on an aureus (gold coin)[25]

The system held while Diocletian was in control. Almost as soon as he and his Western colleague Maximian retired in 305, it began to fracture. A long series of civil wars followed. The conflict was eventually settled when Constantine defeated his last rival in 324 and ruled as sole emperor until his death in 337.

Afterward, however, the divided imperial rule reasserted itself. Constantine preserved the administrative system developed under Diocletian but strengthened the authority of the praetorian prefects, transforming them into senior civilian officials. Over the course of the 4th century, this structure developed into the four great praetorian prefectures of the East, Illyricum, Italy, and Gaul.

The army itself had been changing throughout this period. The *comitatenses* emerged as mobile field armies drawn from soldiers across the empire. They were capable of rapid deployment to a crisis. Provincial armies were reorganized into frontier garrisons known as *limitanei*. They were recruited largely from local populations within the empire and tasked with holding the borders rather than fighting major campaigns. Lactantius, an early Christian writer, claims the total number of soldiers quadrupled under Diocletian, but this is almost certainly an exaggeration. The overall number did increase, but individual unit sizes shrank. More than sixty legions appear to have existed by the end of the 3rd century, but at around a thousand men each rather than the five thousand of the early empire. Cavalry units called *vexillationes* and the older alae and infantry cohorts mustered around five to six hundred men apiece.

Equipment changed too. The rectangular scutum and heavy pilum, the defining equipment of the earlier legionaries, became less common through the 3rd century, replaced by oval shields and lighter spears, such as the lancea. Some units carried lead-weighted darts called plumbatae, slotted into hollows in their shields, up to five per man. Most soldiers wore scale or mail armor and iron helmets. Ammianus, a Roman historian, records Roman infantry raising the *baritus* before battle. This was a Germanic war cry that grew steadily in volume and was used to build courage before an engagement. The adoption of a Germanic battle practice by a Roman army is itself a comment on how much the relationship between Rome and its neighbors had changed.

Tactics varied by theater. Against the Persians in the East, heavily armored cavalry units, the cataphracts and clibanarii, became more prominent in response to the Persian heavy cavalry. Persian archers made advancing at pace more effective than standing to receive the attack, so Eastern engagements more often saw Romans closing quickly rather than holding their ground. In the West, where the main threat was barbarian infantry charges, the opposite approach applied. They were to hold the line in good order, absorb the charge, and then respond from a position of stability.

Through the 4th and 5th centuries, the empire's reliance on foederati, non-Roman tribal groups serving under a treaty, grew steadily. These were different from the traditional auxiliaries. Foederati maintained their own leadership structures, identities, and ways of fighting. They were granted land in exchange for military service, but they were not integrated into the Roman command structure in the same way. They filled gaps that the empire could no longer fill with its own manpower, but in the long term, they were harder to control. Their tribal loyalties took precedence over Roman ones when the two came into conflict.

The crisis point came in 376 CE. A large group of Goths, under pressure from the Huns moving in from the east, asked permission to cross the Danube and settle within the empire. Emperor Valens allowed it. What followed was a catastrophe of Roman administration rather than Gothic aggression. Roman officials exploited and abused the settlers, creating the conditions for revolt.

The resulting conflict ended at the Battle of Adrianople in 378. The size of both armies is uncertain and debated, but the outcome was not. The Romans were destroyed. Emperor Valens probably died on the field, though his body was never recovered; most of his guards had abandoned him during the collapse. Many prominent commanders died alongside him. Survivors escaped during the night. Later writers, including Tyrannius Rufinus, described the battle as the beginning of the empire's troubles, and in retrospect, it is hard to argue with that assessment. It was not that the army was fundamentally broken—it still remained a professional force with real capability—but the defeat forced the empire to depend more on foederati since the losses at Adrianople could not easily be replaced from Roman sources.

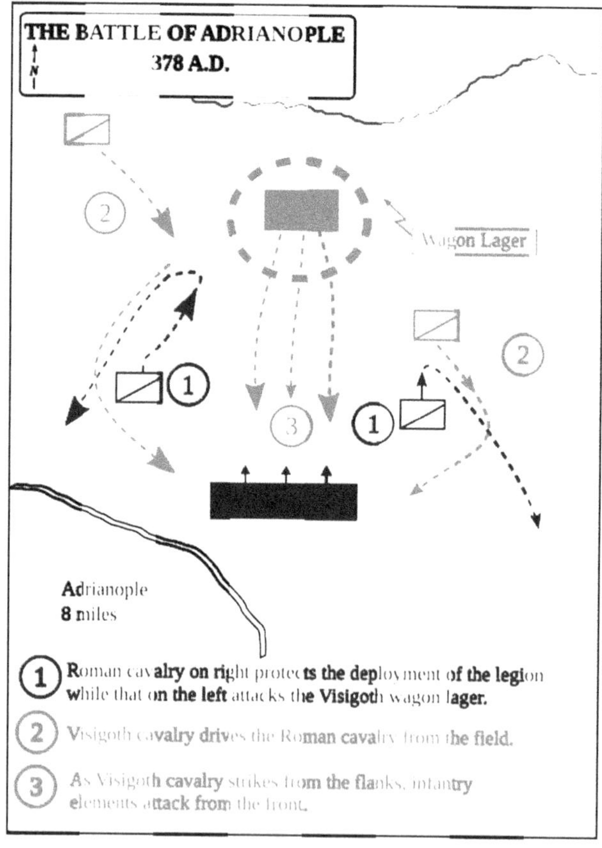

The Battle of Adrianople[26]

By 382, the Goths had accepted peace terms and agreed to provide troops for Rome. The defeat had been severe, but the Roman Empire was still standing. Few people at the time imagined it might actually fall.

One of those Gothic foederati commanders was Alaric. He rose to become king of the Visigoths and spent years seeking formal recognition and land grants from the Western imperial government. Emperor Honorius, ruling from the relative safety of Ravenna, refused to deal with him seriously. Alaric responded by besieging Rome.

The Roman Senate sent envoys to negotiate terms. Alaric's demands were gold, silver, luxury goods, and the release of barbarian slaves. When one envoy asked what would be left for the citizens of Rome, Alaric answered, "Their lives."[i] Rome paid and released the slaves, who promptly joined Alaric's force, making it larger. A second siege followed. A failed attempt by Emperor Honorius to ambush Alaric during negotiations was the end of diplomacy between the two sides. Alaric besieged Rome a third time, and in 410, his forces entered through the Salarian Gate, which had likely been opened by slaves or sympathizers from within.

The sack lasted three days. Looting was extensive, but the violence was restrained by the standards of ancient warfare. There was no mass killing of civilians, and most buildings were left standing. Churches, including St. Peter's Basilica, were left untouched. However, the symbolic damage was enormous. Rome had not been sacked in eight hundred years. The Eternal City, the center of the Roman world, had proven to be neither eternal nor invincible.

Nobles were taken captive, among them the emperor's sister, Galla Placidia. Refugees scattered to Africa, Egypt, and the Eastern provinces. After three days, Alaric left, moving south through Campania, Lucania, and Calabria. He intended to eventually cross to Sicily and Africa. He never got there. He died within months of the sack and was buried, according to legend, with his treasure.

---

[i] Zosimus, *New History*, 2017.

The sack of Rome in 410 by the barbarians[27]

The Visigoths settled in southwestern Gaul in 418 and would later fight alongside Rome against a common enemy from the East. However, the pattern was already clear. Roman victories were becoming rarer and less decisive. The empire was conceding ground it could not recover.

Several barbarian groups, such as the Vandals, Suebi, and Alans, among others, had entered Hispania in 409. The Vandals consolidated control of parts of the peninsula by 420 and then crossed to Africa in 429, seizing large parts of Numidia. In the 430s, Attila unified the Huns and began pushing into the Pannonian and Moesian provinces.

Relations between the Western Roman Empire and the Huns remained workable until around 450. In 451, Attila crossed the Rhine with a large coalition of allied tribes and drove into Gaul. The Western Roman general Flavius Aetius, called "the last of the Romans" by contemporaries, put together a response that was itself a symptom of how much had changed. He assembled an alliance of Romans, Visigoths under Theodoric I, Franks, and Alans. He then met Attila at the Catalaunian Plains.[i]

The fighting was savage, with heavy cavalry charges and close infantry combat. Casualties were enormous. Tens of thousands died, at the very least. Theodoric was killed. His son Thorismund took command of the Visigoths and wanted to press the assault on Attila's camp. Aetius talked him out of it, sending him home to secure the Visigoth throne while applying enough pressure on Attila to force a retreat. It was a calculated decision. The Romans and their allies defeated the Huns enough to stop their advance without destroying them so completely that the balance of power in the region collapsed in unpredictable ways.

Attila retreated, but he was not finished. He turned to Italy, where he continued raiding until 453. He died that year, reportedly on his wedding night. The coalition that had stopped him dissolved almost immediately after. It had been a temporary alignment of interests, not a long-lasting alliance.

Aetius did not survive long either. His political rivalry with Emperor Valentinian III ended with his assassination. After his death, the Western Roman Empire moved faster toward collapse. The Vandal king Gaiseric raided Rome in 455; this was a more systematic plundering than Alaric's sack forty-five years earlier. Between 470 and 490, the Goths absorbed the remaining western provinces in Gaul. In 476, the Germanic commander Odoacer deposed Romulus Augustulus, the last Western Roman emperor, a teenager whose very name combined the founder of Rome with the founder of the empire. Odoacer sent the imperial insignia to Constantinople. The Western Roman Empire was over.

What followed was not a clean break. The Eastern Roman Empire continued, doing so for another thousand years. The new kingdoms that replaced Rome in the West were built on Roman administrative

---

[i] Mesihović, Salmedin, *Orbis Romanvs,* University of Sarajevo, 2015, p. 2407

frameworks, Roman law, and Roman Christianity. The army that had conquered most of the known world left behind something more lasting than the institution itself: a model of organized military power, logistical capability, and disciplined force that shaped European warfare for centuries. The Eastern Roman Empire, Byzantium, carried that inheritance forward, adapting it through a millennium of its own wars and crises. But even in the West, where the legions were gone, the Romans were never entirely gone.

Conclusion

Roman military history is a record of battles, generals, and tactics, but also of a civilization's capacity to adapt and endure. The legions were among the most effective military units of the ancient world, having risen from modest origins to dominance over large parts of Europe, North Africa, and the Near East.

That story has never really left the popular imagination. The French film series *Asterix and Obelix* brought Roman legions, their standards, and their fortified camps to generations of viewers. *Gladiator* gave audiences a Roman general destroyed by the whimsical cruelty of Commodus and thrown into the arena. The TV series *Rome* traced the violent transition from the Roman Republic to the Roman Empire with unusual attention to the military conflicts that drove it. The Romans are everywhere in popular culture and have been for a long time.

It is hard to overstate how central military affairs were to Rome's development from the very beginning. The founding myth itself is a military story. Aeneas, a Trojan warrior, flees the fall of Troy and makes his way to Italy, where his descendants eventually produce Romulus and Remus, who founded the city of Rome. The start of Roman history and the start of Roman military history are pretty much the same moment. What followed across the next twelve centuries shaped the world in ways still visible today. Discipline, training, well-made equipment, and organized logistical support were the practical foundations of Roman military success. However, underlying all of it was flexibility. The same basic structure could be adapted to fight different enemies across radically different terrain, from the forests of Germania to the deserts of North Africa to the hills of Judaea.

That system did not emerge fully formed. Roman warfare began by absorbing Etruscan and Greek practices, adapting the phalanx, and then moving beyond it as the demands of Italian and then Mediterranean conquest required something more versatile. The reforms associated with Gaius Marius accelerated the transition toward a more professional army. He standardized equipment, opened the legions to volunteers regardless of property, and deepened the bond between soldiers and their commanders. That bond had consequences, as the civil wars of the late Roman Republic demonstrated. However, it also produced an army with extraordinary cohesion and endurance. The legions created a model of military organization that outlasted the empire that built them.

Roman military traditions fed into the Byzantine system and moved through Byzantium and other channels into the broader military cultures of medieval Europe. Napoleon Bonaparte consciously adopted Roman symbolism, such as eagle standards for his regiments, the name velites for light infantry units in his guard, and cavalry helmets modeled on Roman designs. The Prussians and Russians put eagles on their flags, and the titles their rulers bore (Kaiser and Tsar) were both derived from Caesar. George S. Patton, one of the most prominent American generals of the Second World War and a serious student of Roman military history, believed he had been a Roman legionary in a previous life. He claimed to remember it while campaigning in Sicily in 1943, retracing ground where Roman armies had fought more than two thousand years before. The term legion itself survives in modern military usage. The French Foreign Legion carries the name, though the connection is symbolic rather than institutional.

Roman road-building and logistical organization set patterns that shaped how later armies thought about supply and movement. The study of Roman campaigns, both their victories and their catastrophic defeats, remains part of military education today. The disasters are analyzed as carefully as the triumphs because the Roman army's failures are as instructive as its successes.

The Roman Empire fell. The causes were multiple and interconnected. There was sustained external pressure, chronic internal political instability, and socio-economic strains that neither discipline nor tactical ingenuity could fully compensate for. However, the military system Rome built proved more durable than the state it served. Its ideas, its organizational logic, its terminology, and its examples passed into the traditions of the armies that came after it, and they are still being studied, argued over, and in some cases imitated today.

Here's another book by Enthralling History that you might like

Free limited time bonus

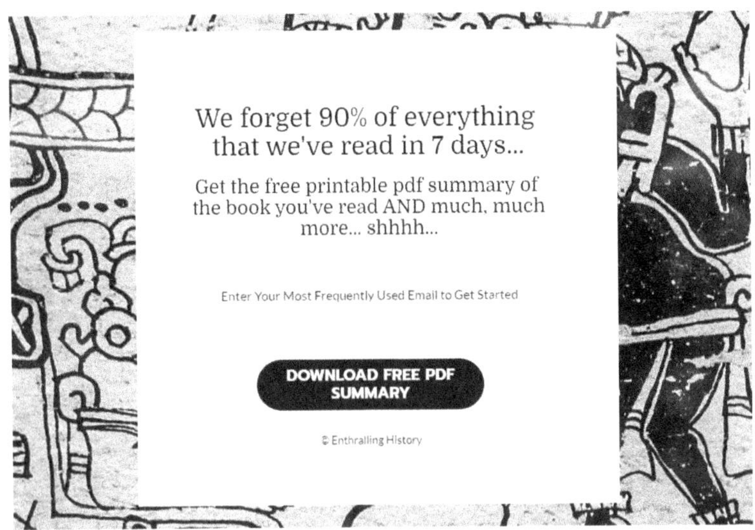

Stop for a moment. We have a free bonus set up for you. The problem is this: we forget 90% of everything that we read after 7 days. Crazy fact, right? Here's the solution: we've created a printable, 1-page pdf summary for this book that you're reading now. All you have to do to get your free pdf summary is to go to the following website:

https://livetolearn.lpages.co/enthrallinghistory/

Or, Scan the QR code!

Once you do, it will be intuitive. Enjoy, and thank you!

Bibliography

Appian, *The Histories,* Loeb Classical Library, 1913.

Dionysius of Halicarnassus, *Roman Antiquities,* Loeb Classical Library, 1940.

Goldsworthy, Adrien, *Roman Warfare,* Wellington House, 2000.

Group of Authors, *Historical Evolution of Roman Infantry, Arms and Armour,* Worcester Polytechnic Institute, 2018.

Harkness, Albert, *The Military System of the Romans,* University of New York, 1887.

Josephus, Flavius, *Wars of the Jews,*

Julius Caesar, *Commentarii De Bello Gallico,* W. J. Gage & Co., 1890.

M. Carry & H. H. Scullard, *A History of Rome down to the Reign of Constantine,* The Macmillan Press Ltd., 1975.

Mashkin, Nikolai, *A History of Ancient Rome,* Gospolitizdat, 1956.

Mesihović, Salmedin, *Orbis Romanvs,* University of Sarajevo, 2015.

Mirković, Miroslava, *Istorija Rimske države,* Službeni glasnik, 2014.

Octavianus Augustus, *Res Gestae divi Augusti,*

Petković, Žarko, *Pad rimske republike,* Filip Višnjić, 2018.

Polybius, *Histories,* Matica Srpska, 1988.

Rostovtzeff, Michael, *A History of the Ancient World: Volume II, Rome,* Oxford University, 1933.

Sallust, *The Jugurthine War and the Conspiracy of Catiline,* Roman Roads Media, 2015.

Titus Livius, *From the Founding of the City,* 2012.

Vegetius, *De re Militari,* University of Nottingham, 1962.

Zosimus, *New History,* 2017.

Image Sources

1   https://commons.wikimedia.org/wiki/File:The_Intervention_of_the_
    Sabine_Women_-_David_(Louvre_INV_3691).jpg

2   https://commons.wikimedia.org/wiki/File:Furius-Camillus.jpg

3 . National Gallery of Art, CC0, via Wikimedia Commons,
    https://commons.wikimedia.org/wiki/File:Pseudo_Melioli,_Romans_Passing_Unde
    r_the_Yoke,_late_15th_-_early_16th_century,_NGA_43922.jpg

4 . Marie-Lan Nguyen / Wikimedia Commons,
    https://commons.wikimedia.org/wiki/File:Pyrrhus_MAN_Napoli_Inv6150_n03.jpg

5 . Piom, translation by Pamela Butler, CC BY-SA 3.0
    <http://creativecommons.org/licenses/by-sa/3.0/>, via Wikimedia Commons,
    https://commons.wikimedia.org/wiki/File:Pyrrhic_War_Italy_en.svg

6 . This image has been created during "DensityDesign Integrated Course Final
    Synthesis Studio" at Politecnico di Milano, organized by DensityDesign Research
    Lab in 2016. Credits goes to Agata Brilli, CC BY-SA 4.0
    <https://creativecommons.org/licenses/by-sa/4.0>, via Wikimedia Commons,
    https://commons.wikimedia.org/wiki/File:Domain_changes_during_the_Punic_Wa
    rs.gif

7   https://commons.wikimedia.org/wiki/File:Corvus_%C3%A4nterbrygga.png

8 . This image has been created during "DensityDesign Integrated Course Final
    Synthesis Studio" at Politecnico di Milano, organized by DensityDesign Research
    Lab in 2016. Credits goes to Agata Brilli, CC BY-SA 4.0
    <https://creativecommons.org/licenses/by-sa/4.0>, via Wikimedia Commons,
    https://commons.wikimedia.org/wiki/File:Domain_changes_during_the_Punic_Wa
    rs.gif

9   https://commons.wikimedia.org/wiki/File:Mommsen_p265.jpg

10 https://commons.wikimedia.org/wiki/File:Scipio_at_the_deathbed_of_
Masinissa_(C20).jpg

11 .This image has been created during "DensityDesign Integrated Course Final
Synthesis Studio" at Politecnico di Milano, organized by DensityDesign Research
Lab in 2016. Credits goes to Agata Brilli, CC BY-SA 4.0
<https://creativecommons.org/licenses/by-sa/4.0>, via Wikimedia Commons
https://commons.wikimedia.org/wiki/File:Domain_changes_during_the_Punic_Wa
rs.gif

12 .José Luiz Bernardes Ribeiro. This file is licensed under the Creative Commons
Attribution-Share Alike 4.0 International license,
https://commons.wikimedia.org/wiki/File:Bust_of_Marius_(GL_319)_-
Glyptothek-_Munich_-_Germany_2017.jpg

13 https://commons.wikimedia.org/wiki/File:Jugurtha_captured.jpg

14 .No machine-readable author provided. MatthiasKabel assumed (based on
copyright claims)., CC BY-SA 3.0 <http://creativecommons.org/licenses/by-sa/3.0/>,
via Wikimedia Commons, https://commons.wikimedia.org
/wiki/File:Roman_aquila.jpg

15 https://commons.wikimedia.org/wiki/File:Retrato_de_Julio_C%C3%A9sar
_(26724093101)_(cropped).jpg

16 https://commons.wikimedia.org/wiki/File:A_Chronicle_of_England_-_Page_005_-
_The_Standard_Bearer_of_the_Tenth_Legion.jpg

17 https://commons.wikimedia.org/wiki/File:Siege-alesia-vercingetorix-jules-cesar.jpg

18 .Vatican Museums, CC BY-SA 4.0 <https://creativecommons.org/licenses/by-
sa/4.0>, via Wikimedia Commons, https://commons.wikimedia.org/wiki
/File:Augustus_of_Prima_Porta_(inv._2290).jpg

19 .ColdEel, CC BY-SA 3.0 <https://creativecommons.org/licenses/by-sa/3.0>, via
Wikimedia Commons, https://commons.wikimedia.org/wiki/File:Roman-Empire-
43BC.png

20 .Cristiano64, CC BY-SA 3.0 <http://creativecommons.org/licenses/by-sa/3.0/>, via
Wikimedia Commons, https://commons.wikimedia.org/wiki/File:
Impero_romano_sotto_Ottaviano_Augusto_30aC_-_6dC.jpg

21 https://commons.wikimedia.org/wiki/File:Otto_Albert_Koch_
Varusschlacht_1909.jpg

22 .CristianChirita, CC BY-SA 3.0 <http://creativecommons.org/licenses/by-sa/3.0/>,
via Wikimedia Commons, https://commons.wikimedia.org/wiki/
File:Engineering_corps_traian_s_column_river_crossing.jpg

23 .NumisAntica, CC BY-SA 3.0 NL <https://creativecommons.org/licenses/by-
sa/3.0/nl/deed.en>, via Wikimedia Commons,
https://commons.wikimedia.org/wiki/File:Romeinse_keizers_Gordianus_III_antoni
nianus_Antiochie_243-244.jpg

24 .FropFrop, CC BY-SA 4.0 <https://creativecommons.org/licenses/by-sa/4.0>, via Wikimedia Commons, https://commons.wikimedia.org/wiki/File: Lorica_segmentata_remains_and_recreation.jpg

25 https://commons.wikimedia.org/wiki/File:5_Aurei,_Diocletian_and_ Maximianus_Herculius,_Elephantenquadriga,_Rome,_287_AD_-_Bode-Museum_-_DSC02724.JPG

26 https://commons.wikimedia.org/wiki/File:Battle_of_Adrianople_378_en.svg

27 https://commons.wikimedia.org/wiki/File:Visigoths_sack_Rome.jpg